LLYN

160 pages of Cai

BEST WALKS

Editor: Osian Pennant Hughes

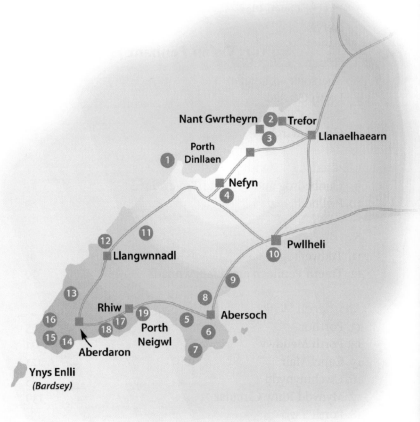

Contents

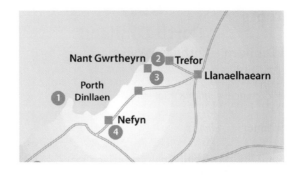

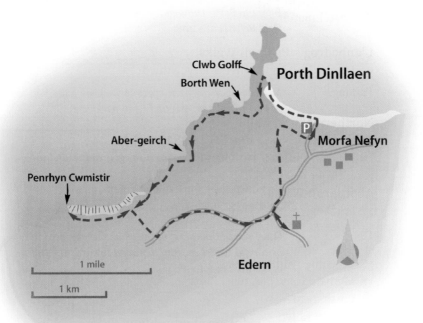

Walk 1
Porth Dinllaen

Walk details

Approx distance: *5 miles/8 kilometres*

Approx time: *3 hours*

O.S. Maps: *1:50 000 Landranger Sheet 123*
1:25 000 Explorer Sheet 253

Start: *Car park at the bottom of the hill from the Golf Club.*
B4412 to Porth Dinllaen
Grid Ref. SH 282 408

Access: *Park, then down Lôn Bridin towards the seaside.*

Parking: *Medium sized car park opposite the Café and Shop at Porth Dinllaen. Around £4 to park here.*

Please note: *Steep steps behind the Tŷ Coch pub.*
Very narrow paths between the golf course and the cliff edge.
Very steep slope down to Borth Wen.
Some wet ground here.

Going: *Quiet road at the start of the walk, but you need to be careful whilst crossing the road towards the end of the walk in Edern.*

It was once famous for its shipbuilding. Over 70 ships were built here, with the last, the 149 ton brigantine *Annie Lloyd*, being launched in 1876. It was also a busy port with 7,000 ships calling here in 1804. Coal was one of the main imports, being stored in Warws Dora on the beach. Local produce was exported from here,

Porth Dinllaen bay

including pigs and butter. In the mid 1800s, there were plans for Porth Dinllaen to be the terminal of the ferry service to Ireland, but the proposal was defeated in parliament by one vote. During the 19th century there was a brickworks here and a landing stage was built on the beach to export the bricks. The Tŷ Coch Inn was, around the 1880s, a naval school kept by a Mrs Jones. The lifeboat station was opened in 1864.

The walk – from Morfa Nefyn over the headland to Borth Wen and Aber-geirch bays and then inland to the village of Edern and back along various paths to Morfa Nefyn.

Walk directions
Park your car in the National Trust car park near the Golf Club in Morfa Nefyn and walk up the hill towards

the Golf Club. Go down the road that runs through the golf course to the shed on the left. There is an unmarked public footpath here across the green to the edge of the cliff – but watch the golf balls! Once you reach the cliff edge, go to your left and follow the path.

At the end of the golf course you will reach a stile near a hut. Go over it and down to Borth Wen where a pipe runs to the sea. Cross the footbridge and follow the path up a hill to an old gate. As it won't open, go over it carefully and then bear right keeping to the path that runs above the cliff.

Continue towards a kissing gate, and onto Aber-geirch. Here there is a signpost. Take the path down to the small bay, over a footbridge and then up the steep steps and continue to another kissing gate. Go through it and continue along the footpath.

Walk down into the bay where there is another signpost, cross the stream, and then up the steep steps to

Aber-geirch

The coastal village of Porth Dinllaen

a kissing gate and follow the path above the cliff. Cross another stream to a kissing gate and to a signpost and a gate. Go through the gate and walk inland along the track. If it is wet, you might have to walk on the old bank running alongside it. Continue to a farm gate with a farm on the right. Go through the gate and continue to a road. Turn left and follow the road to the crossroads at Edern near the chapel.

Turn left and walk down towards the pub, over the bridge, up the hill and around the bend where you will see on your left an iron kissing gate. Go through it and up the left hand side of the field and then down to a gate and kissing gate. Go through the kissing gate, across the track to another kissing gate and up the left hand side of the field to another kissing gate. Continue past the Nefyn Golf Club on your left, down the hill and back to the car park.

If you're feeling thirsty, why not visit the Tŷ Coch Inn on the beach and taste the local brew, Cwrw Llŷn?

Walk out of the car park and turn left and then left again down Lôn Bridin and to the beach. Turn left and walk along the sand towards the houses. A path goes behind the houses which takes you to another beach at Porth Dinllaen where the inn is.

Take this lane, 'Lôn Bridin' down to the beach

You can either return this way, or follow the path behind the inn until you come to a track and then turn left and up the narrow road that crosses the golf course and then downhill to the car park.

Other Points of Interest
Aber-geirch From here at one time an undersea telephone cable ran to Ireland. It was about three

Go up these steps behind the Tŷ Coch pub on Porth Dinllaen beach

inches thick, and during the First World War was guarded by soldiers.

Borth Wen was where the *Arjon* from Germany and her crew were all lost in a huge storm in 1863. The villagers, watching the drama unfold from the clifftop, could do nothing to help. The cargo of three ships came ashore here after that storm and the local minister had to warn his flock not to help themselves to the goods.

Tŷ Coch Inn on the beach at Porth Dinllaen

Porth Dinllaen RNLI This station houses an inshore lifeboat and it is also a dock for the local coastguard. With its north facing bay, Porth Dinllaen used to be an

The RNLI boathouse at Porth Dinllaen

important harbour of refuge and a busy port – over 700 ships passed through the port in 1861. The boat shed and slip were commissioned in 1864 and manned constantly since. A new visitor centre is opening on this site.

Porth Dinllaen Heritage Centre The National Trust and Llŷn Area of Outstanding

Natural Beauty (AONB) have a display at a small heritage centre at the head of the beach during summer.

Originally published in
National Trust Walks 1. Northern Wales

by Dafydd Meirion

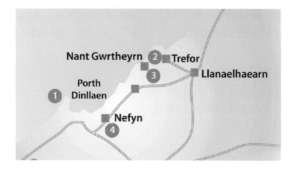

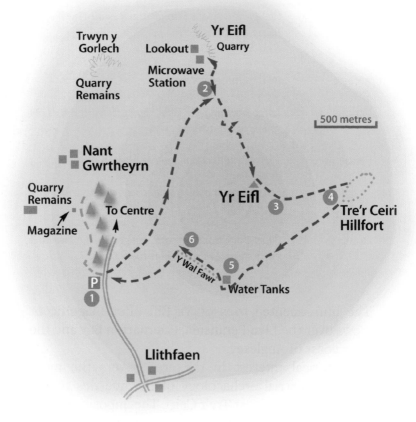

Walk 2
Yr Eifl

Walk details
Approx distance: *5 miles/8 kilometres*

Approx time:	*3 hours*
O.S. Maps:	*1:50 000 Landranger Sheet 123* *1:25 000 Explorer Sheet 253*
Start:	*Car park between Llithfaen and Nant Gwrtheyrn.* *B4417 Llithfaen/Nefyn* *Grid Ref. SH 353 439*
Access:	*B4417 Llithfaen/Nefyn*
Parking:	*Large free car park before going down towards the village of Nant Gwrtheyrn.*
Please note:	*Very wet and muddy ground between points 2 and 3 on the map.* *Steep climb at point 3 and between points 2 and 3 on the map.*
Going:	*Quiet track from car park, but gets muddy, wet and fairly steep towards the off-road paths.*

The unfrequented tops of Yr Eifl offer magnificent views over the Llŷn Peninsula, Caernarfon Bay and the west coast of Anglesey.

Historical interest in the area covers the more recent industrial archaeology of the quarries to the Bronze Age fortress at Tre'r Ceiri. The imposing quarry of Yr Eifl once exported its product via the jetty in

Yr Eifl above Llithfaen

Trefor. This in itself was not unusual as most quarries in the area relied on sea transport to move the goods to a market. However, Yr Eifl quarry transported the stone to the jetty in Trefor by means of an aerial cable way. Eddie Doylerush in his book on aircraft crashes during the Second World War tells of an incident involving this cable. On 9 September, 1943 an Avro Anson from the No.3 Air Gunnery School based at Mona was on a training flight. The pilot was putting the aircraft through its paces near the Eifl quarries and inadvertently clipped the cable with the port wing of the plane. The Anson, now out of control plunged into the sea. Three aircraftmen survived the crash and two tragically died.

Also locally is Nant Gwrtheyrn, an old quarry village now used as a centre for Welsh culture. The centre is involved in the preservation of the Welsh language and

The remains of the Brythonic village at Tre'r Ceiri

offers courses for beginners and academics alike. Nant Gwrtheyrn also has links with Welsh folklore. Its name can be translated as Vortigern's ravine, and is reputed to be the last resting place of Vortigern. His name is always linked with that of Merlin, with whom he had many adventures. One of the most famous was the conflict with the dragons at Dinas Emrys near Beddgelert. In a later conflict Vortigern retreated to Nant Gwrtheyrn after a battle with the Jutes under the command of Hengist and Horsa. He was accused of betraying his country to the enemy and came here to die.

Undoubtedly the most important historical feature in the area is the magnificent Bronze Age hillfort at Tre'r Ceiri (Village of the Giants). Said to be the largest Bronze Age hillfort in the British Isles, the site was in occupation up until AD 78. The inner walls enclose an area of about 5 acres on which are situated over 100 huts. The Cytiau (huts) are situated in groups scattered on the terraces and slopes inside the fort. The huts themselves conform to no particular pattern and can be round, oval, oblong and even rectangular. The walls of the huts were crudely built, being about 4ft thick and 3 to 4ft high. This must have led to very cramped living conditions even where huts had two linked chambers. Archaeologists have found remains on the site which paint a colourful history. Roman, British and Celtic pottery has been found as well as porcelain beads from Egypt. The nature of the finds and the location of the site would indicate that the fortress was only occupied during the summer season. The lack of charcoal remains would indicate that fires

Path leading up to the Eifl from the car park

were not used on the site. This would seem to confirm its use as a summer site, as it is unlikely that the inhabitants would have been without fires in the damp and cold winters.

Walk directions

1.   Turn right out of the car park and then left up large track towards col.

2.   Just after the top of the rise a gate is seen on the left. One of the summits lies this way. Pass through the gate and towards the microwave station, round the station keeping close to the fence at the north-western corner to

This path leads up to the first of three trigs on the Eifl

The spectacular view. northwards from the summit – towards Caernarfon, the Menai Strait and Anglesey

pick up and ascend an ancient stairway to the summit and lookout. However as no right of way exists and due to the presence of a locked gate this diversion is not recommended. Return to the col by the same route. Cross track and

Follow this path until you reach the third trig of the Eifl – as seen in the distance

straight up to the summit. Ignore all crossing tracks and keep to direct path which steepens as it crosses some scree just before the summit. At the Trig point turn to face in the direction of the path by which you ascended. A vague path ½ right will be seen going in the direction of Tre'r Ceiri.

On the third trig, there is a well-preserved Iron Age hillfort and a heritage information board.

3. Follow this descending track and after initial steep drop go through a wall gap and across moor by means of vague tracks to reach gap in fortified wall.

4. Through gap and follow path to summit. Descend from summit and follow path south west through a

A southwards view from the hillfort, towards the coast of Llŷn and Bae Ceredigion

different wall gap and on to a kissing gate. Follow path to a second kissing gate and pass to the right hand path upwards.

5. Follow track for 25 metres. Look out for narrow path running alongside remains of an old wall on your left.

6. Follow this to a crossing path then left on path and return to car park.

Refreshments Café in Nant Gwrtheyrn, and Café and in Llanaelhaearn and Tafarn y Fic village pub in Llithfaen.

Originally published in
From Mountain Tops to Valley Floors

by Dave Salter and Dave Worrall

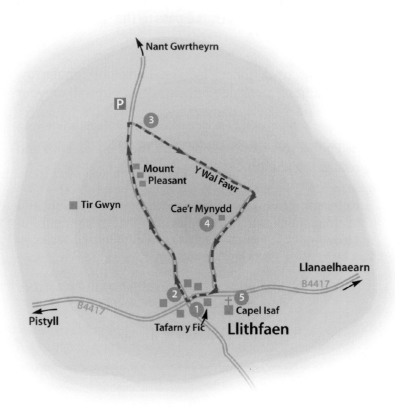

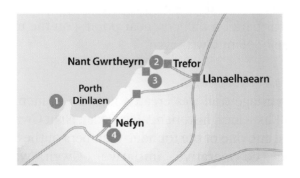

Walk 3
Llwybr Gwyn Plas

Walk details

Approx distance: *1½ miles/2.4 kilometres*

Approx time:	*45 minutes*
O.S. Maps:	*1:50 000 Landranger Sheet 123* *1:25 000 Explorer Sheet 253*
Start:	*Llithfaen. B4417 to Llithfaen* *Grid Ref. SH 357 432*
Access:	*From Caernarfon to Pwllheli. Near the roundabout,* *turn right towards Nefyn.*
Parking:	*Roadside by 'Tafarn y Fic' public house in Llithfaen* *or in the pass at the top of Nant Gwrtheyrn.*
Please note:	*Rather wet path by 'Y Wal Fawr'.*
Going:	*Quiet roads up and down hill, open pasture footpath.*

Park at the back of 'Tafarn y Fic' public house in the village of Llithfaen, or turn upwards at the Llithfaen crossroad towards Nant Gwrtheyrn and park in the large car park on the left (near point 3 on the map) at the top of Nant Gwrtheyrn.

Walk significance

This heritage trail was created in 2009 in memory of Gwyn Elis, a local historian, walk leader, Nant Gwrtheyrn trustee and one of the founder-members of the 'Tafarn y Fic' co-operative initiative. Gwyn was an

*Gwyn Elis, leading a walking party around Llithfaen, appreciating
the countryside and also the local history and heritage*

inspirational character, enjoying every aspect of his
heritage.

The path links with other paths in the area – Llŷn
coastal path, Pilgrim's route, Eifl and Tre'r Ceiri – and
can be used as an approach to longer walks.

Walk directions

*Park near 'Tafarn y Fic', which is the
village's local pub*

As this is a circular village
walk, you can join it as you
like. There are six heritage
stones on route and are
numbered on the map.

From 'Tafarn y Fic', take
the right turning towards Nant
Gwrtheyrn. When you reach a
large car park, look out for a
sign on the right signposted
'Llwybr Gwyn Plas'. Take this

route, keeping the wall to your right. Pass a large crop of trees, until you come to a gate and a white house on your right. Go through the gate, and walk down the lane. When you reach the main road, you will be faced with a chapel. Turn right and you will be back in the village where you parked.

1. **Tafarn y Fic** was built in 1869. In 1988, local people created a co-operative company to buy the pub, which had by then closed its doors. It became a lively social centre, renowned for its Welsh music nights, and serves the local real ales, brewed by Cwrw Llŷn. The building was modernised and extended in 2004 creating a community room, Y Daflod restaurant, as well as continuing as a Welsh pub.
www.tafarnyfic.com
www.ydaflod.com

2. **Y Groes, Llithfaen**
Llithfaen was a granite quarrying community, and the road from Y Groes (crossroads) to the coastal quarries would have been full of workers walking through all kinds of weather to the rock faces.

Llithfaen is a traditional granite quarrymen's village

Granite setts were exported by steamboats to face city roads and pavements. There was a strong tradition of co-operative businesses under workers' control at Llithfaen.

The Quarrymen's memorial at the car park above Nant Gwrtheyrn

Cofio Chwarelwyr Llithfaen *Quarrymen's memorial* A memorial sculpture in granite stands near the car park above Nant Gwrtheyrn in memory of the quarrymen of the three western Eifl quarries.

3. Y Wal Fawr This long and high perimeter wall was built by unemployed soldiers returning from Waterloo. The square fields below the wall were marked out by surveyors – this is the land that was legally stolen by the estate landowners from the traditionally shared community common ground by the Eifl Enclosure Act. It is estimated that over a million acres – a fifth of the country – was enclosed by London parliamentary acts.

4. Cae'r Mynydd Using a large sea shell, Robert William Hughes of Cae'r Mynydd called on the people

The ruin of Robert William Hughes' cottage, Cae'r Mynydd

of Llithfaen to resist the officials and land-measurers in September 1812. A riot followed and a troop of Dragoons was sent to Llithfaen to capture the ringleaders. Robert Hughes was caught hiding in the rafters of his cottage and was sentenced to be hanged, but was 'pardoned' and sent to Botany Bay for the rest of his life.

The Welsh language and heritage centre of Nant Gwrtheyrn

5. Capel Isaf Llithfaen's population swelled with the growth of the Eifl granite quarries – a larger Methodist chapel was built every 20 years during the 1800s. The last chapel was opened in 1905 with a unique circular gallery for a choir behind the pulpit. Llithfaen was renowned throughout Wales for its choir singing tradition and Llithfaen Male Voice Choir won the main competition at the National Eisteddfod in 1925 and 1945.

6. Eglwys Carnguwch The history of Carnguwch church, which is consecrated to Beuno, an early Welsh saint, dates back to the 7th century. It is located on a secluded mount above Afon Erch and is now in the care of a group of local volunteers.

Originally published as a leaflet:
Llwybr Gwyn Plas
Llwybr Treftadaeth Llithfaen/ Llithfaen Heritage Trail

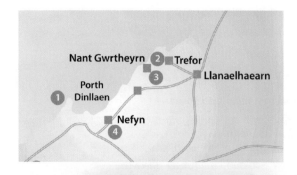

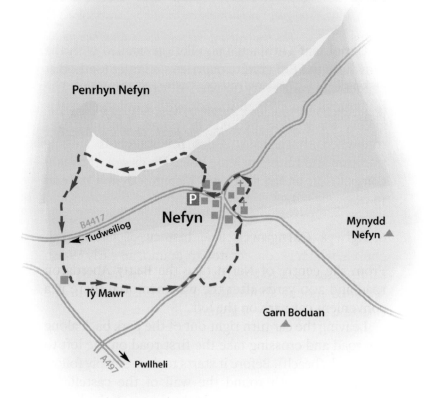

Walk 4
Nefyn

Walk details

Approx distance: *3½ miles/5.6 kilometres*

Approx time:	*1¾ hours*
O.S. Maps:	*1:50 000 Landranger Sheet 123*
	1:25 000 Explorer Sheet 253
Start:	*Car park next to the Police Station.*
Access:	*The road leading down to the beach. Then up the path by a building which looks like a castle.*
Parking:	*Public car park (next to the Police Station).*
Please note:	*High cliff path at first ½ mile of the walk around the bay, which is above the beach. There is no fence here therefore care is needed!*
Going:	*A busy main road at the start of the walk by the car park.*

Walk directions

From the centre of Nefyn take the B4417 Aberdaron road and 200 yards after the war memorial there is a convenient car park on the left.

Leaving the car turn right out of the park back along the road and crossing take the first road on the left to the *traeth* (beach). Before it starts to drop steeply follow the cliff top path round the wall of the castellated house on the left. The path looks down on the beach, where at one time, ships would unload their cargo into

Above Nefyn beach, looking towards Porth Nefyn headland

carts pulled by horses; now holiday makers take advantage on the 1½ miles of sand to swim and sail.

Above the tiny harbour a landslip has caused the path to be diverted through a kissing gate onto what is

Looking back down towards Nefyn beach, with the Eifl mountain range in the distance

a drive to a private house. After 50 yards look out for a rough, narrow, overgrown lane on the left. This leads to a cluster of cottages round a pond. Follow the rough access road between the two cottages in front and in 100 yards or so come out onto the main road.

One of the country lanes that you meet after descending the coastal path

Crossing the road follow the footpath sign alongside the house directly opposite. Going straight ahead, through two kissing gates, over two wooden stiles and then a farm gate keep to the left of this field to find another kissing gate at the far end by the farm Tŷ Mawr. Keeping the farm on the right go through another gate beside the farmhouse and immediately turn left through a small rickety wooden gate down a narrow path which leads, after a few yards and an overgrown pond to another kissing gate and slate slab bridge. Keeping to the right of this field make for the stile at the far side and then bearing left enter a very overgrown farm lane which, after 100 yards, comes out onto the access lane to the farm on the left. Go through the gate immediately in front keeping to the left of the field to find a wooden stile in the corner.

Negotiate this and immediately turn right to follow up the side of the field. Just beyond the house on the right go through a kissing gate onto the main road.

Turn left and after 50 yards cross to the lay-by on the

Garn Boduan above Nefyn

opposite side. A yard or two further on go through a kissing gate on the right and head across the field with Garn Boduan directly in front keeping just to the right of the gorse patch. When the bottom of the valley comes into view veer off left down to the bottom where there are signs of a rough track leading across the wet valley and up the other side. Instead of crossing to the other side however look out for two or three shallow stone steps on the left up onto a low grass embankment by the finger post. Keep along the top of the embankment until a kissing gate is reached. Passing through don't take the path going up to the right but head towards the houses in front keeping to the right of the field. This is possibly the site of Edward's tournament in 1284. Another kissing gate leads onto a drive and then out onto the road.

Turn left into the village and after passing the Baptist chapel, the bakery and a row of cottages take the first street on the right. This leads through the old part of Nefyn to the old church with its distinctive sailing ship weather vane. The church is no longer used as such but has been turned into a very interesting maritime museum with particular emphasis on Nefyn and its seafaring tradition. Unfortunately the museum is only open during the main season.

Take the narrow street opposite the church entrance and then turn left on the main road through the village. Just before the mini-roundabout in the centre notice St Mary's well on the right; a never failing supply of water for pilgrims and villagers in days gone by.

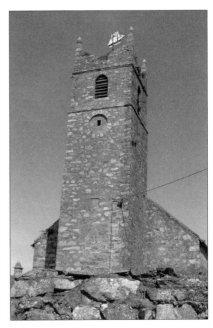

St Mary's, Nefyn – now a maritime heritage centre

Turning right see the old look out tower on the right just before the new church. Continue along the road, pass the village hall, war memorial and school to arrive back at the car park.

Originally published in
Llŷn Peninsula Coastal Walks

by Richard A. R. Quine

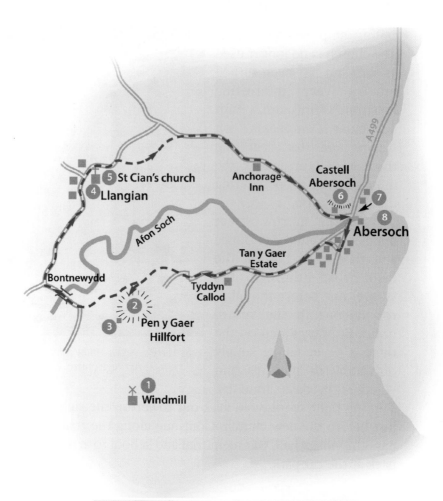

Walk 5
Abersoch – Llangian

Walk details

Approx distance: *3 miles/4.8 kilometres*

Approx time:	*2 hours*
O.S. Maps:	*1:50 000 Landranger Sheet 123* *1:25 000 Explorer Sheet 253*
Start:	*Abersoch. Grid Ref. SH 315 282*
Access:	*Go past Ysgol Abersoch, turning left at the bottom of the road towards Llanengan.*
Parking:	*In Abersoch. The car park is by the golf course and the primary school, but you need to pay.*
Please note:	*The walk around Pen-y-gaer is fairly steep but is quite easy.* *The cob between Pen-y-gaer and Llangian runs along land that can get flooded during the wet season.*
Going:	*Quiet lanes. Follow the grassy path along the side of 'Pen-y-gaer' until you reach the long bridge leading to Porth Neigwl and Llangian.*

The following walk is an ideal pre-lunch or pre-dinner walk and takes you through pretty scenery, passing through one of the most 'awarded' villages on Llŷn, Llangian, with its beautiful church and sheltered setting it seems a long way from the twentieth century.

The busy resort of Abersoch

Afon Soch estuary

A start as good as any is from the St Tudwals, the public house in the centre of the village. Walk up the main street until the turn off on the right. Take this road which goes past the village hall. The road is called Lôn Gwydryn. At the T-junction at the bottom of the hill take the road signposted Llanengan heading left uphill.

The road, after a few hundred metres and another short rise, bends to the left but you carry straight on, the first house on the left after joining this road is called 'Derwyn', another house is on the right called 'Derwin' therefore **do not** go that way. On the right is a sign outside a small estate called Tan-y-gaer (*gaer* :

fort), which is a reference to the hillfort which we will pass further up the lane.

Turn left, pass a broken pine tree on a bend and there you'll observe an unusual house 'Tyddyncallod'. The fort you are heading towards is visible through the trees and undergrowth, straight ahead on top of a hill. Come to a fork and take the right path through a gate with the name Brongaer. The road now runs straight for about 200 metres. Keep your eyes peeled around here for gold finches (1).

This private looking lane is actually part of the Public Footpath

Head towards the gate in front of you through the kissing gate on the left, keep to the wall on the left after passing through the gate. Walk on through the lane lined with gorse bushes – this is worth seeing in June. There is a valley ahead with the village of Llangian in its depth. Mynydd Rhiw is visible in the distance.

A detour is possible here, going up to the fort (2) on top of the hill. There is very little of the fort left to see, but the view from the top is worth the effort. If detouring, turn left after passing through the gate posts and head up the path to the summit, reached in a hundred and fifty metres or so.

Retrace your steps to the gate posts and return to your route.

If you walk to the outer edge of the path in the

A view of Llangian village, as seen from Pen-y-gaer

direction of Garn Fadryn, you will see approx. 20 metres in front of you at the bottom of a grassy slope a small marshy area. This is the site of an ancient well and may have been the water source for the inhabitants of the hillfort Pen-y-gaer you have just visited.

The path which descends down from Pen-y-gaer towards the road

Follow the steep track (not too steep) down the side of the hill (3).

Ahead of you is a gate, go through this and proceed down the hillside, where, on your right is an impressive stand of reeds (*Phragmites autralis*). These were used for good quality thatching, although because of its abundance locally, bracken was extensively used.

There are stone steps set in the wall bordering the road; these are visible when you are approaching the road.

Go up on to the road and turn right towards Llangian. The marshy land to the left of the road floods extensively in winter, which is why there is a bridge over this area. This bridge is called Bontnewydd and divides the parishes of Llanengan and Llangian and replaced Edmund Hyde-Hall's 'bridge of three arches'. At the centre of the bridge is a plaque that tells you what vehicles may cross it and the weight restrictions – strange getting a warning when you are already halfway across the bridge! In about 200 metres you will come upon a signpost, Porth Neigwl (*Hell's Mouth*) to left, Llangian to right in ½ mile (4).

The cob at Llangian, which is likely to flood during heavy rainfall

Vintage roadsign in Llangian village

In a few dozen yards you will see the church of St Cian, if you have time, it is well worth a look around (5).

On the ascent of the hill heading towards Abersoch, on the first bend, our signposted footpath breaks off the road to the right and is the way to proceed, enter through the gate into a tunnel of trees and undergrowth. Carry on to the next gate, go straight through and walk on up the slope. The view to the right is of the village of Llangian and the churchyard, while beyond that stretches the wide sweep of Porth Neigwl (*Hell's Mouth*). After a few hundred metres you will join the main road, turn right and follow this back into Abersoch.

Visible from the road at this point and looking right you will gain a good view of the fort visited earlier. At around this time you could well be in need of some refreshment, if so, then on your right is the 'Anchorage Inn' open all day and with some good views from the bar.

The harbour breakwater visible in the distance, built in 1924, now appears directly in front of you with the Pen Benar headland behind it. Follow the road for approx. ¼ of a mile and then you will be entering Abersoch. When you reach the village and the main road, on your left there is a garage and boat salesroom, called 'Abersoch Land & Sea' (6). Turn right here and head back into the village centre.

On your left as you walk along the main road is an area known as the 'Green' but is in fact filled with sea water at high tide, this is the winter resting place of many of the local boats. At low water look out for the resident heron, fishing for the many eels which abound in this river (7) (8).

Just before reaching the village centre there are public toilets on your left.

History notes
1. On your left, just visible through the trees and about two fields away is the remains of an old windmill. This would have been the place where the inhabitants of Llanengan would have brought their corn, etc, to be milled by the resident miller for the cost of a few pence. This mill was already in a ruinous condition by the early 1800s.

2. On arriving at the summit take in the scenery for a few minutes. The fort itself is of oval structure, the

remains of the entrance lies to the north east. This fortified hamlet or family settlement was occupied by a wave of Iron Age settlers sometime around 100 BC. It was thought to contain two stone-built round huts, together accommodating no more than 12 to 20 people. It may have been one large family or a couple of smaller families that had united as a 'tribe'. The occupants would have been agriculturalists growing cereal-type crops. They would probably have had a few cows and sheep and maybe goats. With the close proximity of the sea they would undoubtedly have supplemented their diet with fresh fish.

It was probably the Romans who put an end to the occupation of this site. The 23rd Legion, based at Segontium (Caernarfon) were occasionally active in Llŷn. Indeed, there is evidence that most of the population of the area that were either living in small hill top forts like this one or in lowland hut groups, were 'rounded up' and forced to live in one of three large 'reservation' type communities on top of Garn Fadryn (visible north), Tre'r Ceiri (also visible north) and Garn Boduan.

3. The exposed rock face on your left is the remains of a quarry, higher up this hill there are some exploratory mine workings that go back into the hill directly under the fort. This took place in 1835 and was a joint venture by John Greaves and Samuel Holland, both these men were major slate mine owners in the Ffestiniog area. They were also prime-movers in the development of the slate shipping trade as well as the subsequent development of Porthmadog harbour: where both Greaves' and Holland's wharfs can be seen. They were mining here for lead and iron ore, the iron was sent to

Cardiff. It was not deemed sufficiently remunerative for these two gentlemen and the workings were soon abandoned. The excavation may have taken place to extend the lead mine on Trwyn Cilan.

4. The house facing you as you enter the village is Sgubor Ddegwm. This is the site of the old village tithe barn. Llangian has had awards for the best kept village in Wales at least once and that was in 1964, plaques commemorating this and others are displayed outside the church hall on a post.

Up until the early part of this century, Llangian boasted its own smithy, which was situated opposite 'Capel Smyrna' which is the nonconformist chapel on your left. This is architecturally, slightly more ornate than is usually seen in this type of building.

The large house on the left with tall red brick chimneys is called Ty'n Llan.

Llangian village was the birth place in 1540, of a famous Welsh poet, Wiliam Owen, known as 'Wiliam Llŷn'.

5. The church has a noteworthy 15th century roof, the walls of local rubble have been rebuilt and all openings as well as the west bell-cote, are modern. On the south wall may be seen some original footing boulders, dating from the later 13th century. The church was extended in the 15th century when the present roof was constructed and is now unusually long. The roof is of arch-braced and collar beam type and is supported by ten trusses resting on modern wall posts and stone corbels. A nice architectural feature is a cross set in contrasting stone above the porch.

In the churchyard to the south is a table-tomb to

Llangian church

John Williams of Ty'n-y-coed, Dr and Minister 1673 (in Latin). A much more ancient 'doctor' is also buried in this churchyard. A few feet to the south west of the church door is a rough stone pillar with three holes visible in the top, this is thought to have been a support for a sundial. On one side of the pillar and barely visible (acid rain has caused rapid recent degeneration) an inscription which reads downwards: *Meli Medici/Fili Martini/Iacit*. This translates as 'Melus the doctor, son of Martinus he lies (here)'. This stone is of 5th or early 6th century and reflects a continuance of some sort of Roman way of life after the departure of the legions in AD 410. This stone is of particular importance in that reference to the professional occupation of laymen are extremely rare. In the Christian inscriptions within Britain, the term *medicus* does not occur on any other monument.

On leaving the church and facing west, there always

used to be a ship's figurehead on a cottage near the T-junction at the village centre. This was hanging outside but unfortunately, is now in place only in the summer season. If you are here in the summer the profusion of flowers decorating this beautiful village, combined with its secluded pastoral setting, must make it one of the prettiest in Llŷn.

6. As you reach the main road by the side of 'Land and Sea' and look in that direction, past and behind the houses alongside, you will notice a fairly high raised bank, the seaward end of which is cut through by the present road. This bank is the remains of the outer rampart of an earthwork castle. This was situated on top of the bank and occupied the area where the modern housing estate next to the old 'White House Hotel' now stands. This earthwork castle is an example of what is known as a 'motte and bailey' castle. This consisted of a keep or motte on a raised mound, surrounded by the roughly circular area of the bailey also raised like a plateau above the surrounding area which contained other buildings such as kitchens, stables, storehouses etc. The area of the bailey would be surrounded by a wooden palisade. All these buildings, including the keep or motte would have been timber, only later would this timber keep have been replaced by a stone one.

Castles of this type date from around the middle of the 12th century, a time when Wales was experiencing aggressive incursions from the Normans who had recently conquered England. North-western Wales was subject to invasions throughout the 12th century, from the Chester area.

The motte and bailey castle is the classic Norman

fortification, often hastily erected in newly conquered areas in an attempt to maintain control over the district. However, it is thought that the native Welsh leaders may have copied this motte and bailey style of fortification in response to the Norman invader, consequently it is not often possible to tell if a site such as 'Castell Abersoch' is a Norman outpost or a native Welsh stronghold.

It is reported that a few 'stone hammers' were found here when it was cut through to make the road.

7. Behind the 'Green', is the lifeboat station, (re-built in 1994). Adjacent to this and across to the arches are some of the oldest buildings in Abersoch. This is the site of the old boatyard where sailing craft were built. There were 14 vessels constructed here between 1774 and 1854, typical of these were the *Penrhyn* (a vessel of 76 tons) and the *New Blessing* (92 tons) both these craft were built in 1811 and were registered in Pwllheli.

8. Aber-soch used to be a small fishing village with just a few cottages. It has a fine maritime tradition and when the tourist industry grew during the 20th century, it became a popular holiday resort.

Selection of original walk, originally published in:
Walks in the Llŷn Peninsula
Part 1: South and West

by N. Burras and J. Stiff

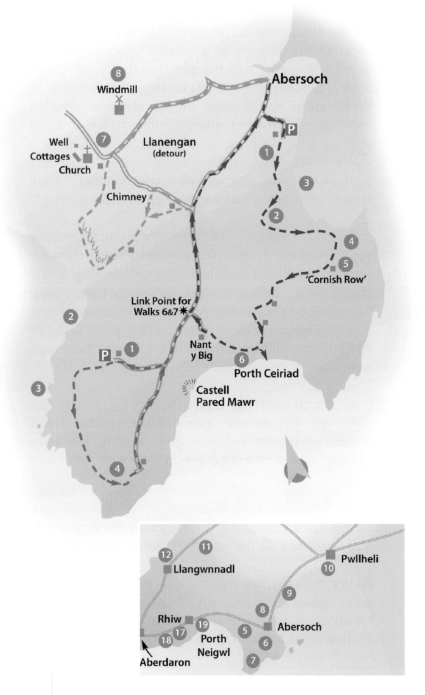

Walk 6
Abersoch – Porth Ceiriad

Walk details
Approx distance: *6½ miles/10.5 kilometres (full journey)*

Approx time:	*3 hours*
O.S. Maps:	*1:50 000 Landranger Sheet 123* *1:25 000 Explorer Sheet 253*
Start:	*Abersoch. Grid Ref. SH 315 282*
Access:	*A499 into Abersoch.*
Parking:	*A car park (with a charge) on the way down towards the golf course.*
Please note:	*Steep steps down towards Porth Ceiriad.* *Uneven road past the remains of an old quarry.*
Going:	*Quiet lane during the first half of the walk.* *Busy road during the end if you decide to walk alongside the main road from Sarn Bach back to Abersoch.* *A mixture of tarmac, stony and grassy roads.*

Quite a mixture, from lead mines to a sheltered cove on the tip of a headland, if you include the detour it is quite a tiring walk but one you'll always remember.

As before in the Pen-y-gaer walk, St Tudwals Inn is as good a place to start as any. Head up the main street for about 150 metres or so and turn left into Lôn Golff. (Follow signs to Golf Club.)

The inner harbour at Abersoch, during a warm summer's day

At the large car park make a right turn into the road leading to the golf links and follow the signs for the golf course (1).

When you have reached the club house continue across the links, this track is quite long, about ½ mile.

The road forks to the right near the end of the links, take this fork and continue down the stony track. After a while and a short rise, connect with a tarmacadam surface and turn left (2).

One of the many unusual footpath crossings from the golf course

Follow this footpath until it emerges onto a road, cross this and continue along the path. Keep an eye open here for the birdlife that feeds on the mud flats in front of the old lifeboat station, several species are represented: turnstones, oyster catchers, redshanks, dunlins and assorted ducks etc., tide allowing (3).

At the sharp bend in the lane, turn right up the hill and follow the path, this is very stony and very wet, it is like this in summer and winter alike and after a heavy storm it's more like a river. As you go up this road you will notice on your left the spoil heaps and remains of mine workings (4).

The path which goes inland, with the sea behind you

Continue up the hill and after 100 metres or so you will see on your left the old pumping station for the mine.(5).

Carry on along this route until you pass an area on your right containing spoil from the mine, this area is private, so best stick to the path. On your left is a farm, Penrhyn Mawr.

Remains of the mine workings

A little further up the road on the same side you will see some low ruined walling, this area may have been covered by a large storage/sorting house.

As the road swings to the right and becomes a hard surface there is a house on your left, but behind it runs

Go through this kissing gate and into a large open field

This path passes a caravan park, then leads down to Porth Ceiriad

The grassy path, with the waters of Porth Ceiriad in the distance

Take a left turn here, and down to Porth Ceiriad beach

the next section of footpath. Turn onto the garden by the hedge and walk through the large boulders which mark the perimeter of the garden, one of these is pure quartz. Ascend the steps beside the house, the footpath then passes through a field.

Walk along the field keeping the fence on your right, follow this path around the edge of the fields, admiring the scenery as you go, until you reach a kissing gate – just in front of Cim farmhouse – go through this and walk on, keeping the fence to your right.

On your left, in the garden of the farmhouse is a 19th century well-head pump. Go past the farmhouse, then around the green in front of you keeping the face to your left. Go all the way around it until you see a kissing gate to your right that leads into the field.

Continue along this track until you reach another stile – a house just to the right of this field approx. 50 metres is called Crowrach – cross over and go through a gap on your left, head diagonally across the field heading towards the next stile, cross this and continue

The secret beach of Porth Ceiriad on the western tip of Trwyn Cilan

along the field until you reach yet another stile which leads onto a road. On your right is a cattle grid, but you need to turn left here and walk down the lane, where, in about 50 metres the lane forks, take the right fork and head towards the caravans in front of you.

The track runs to the left of the caravans. Follow it through the gate down a narrow path.

When you come to the fork, take the left one towards the beach Porth Ceiriad (6). On reaching the kissing gate which leads onto the beach you will have a choice, if you go down to the beach you will now be on one of the most delightful beaches in Llŷn as it is very sheltered and has plenty of good sand, there's usually room for everybody to sit as it is about ½ mile long. Good surfing and fishing (mainly for skate) or just plain sunbathing.

For those wishing to continue the walk, turn right and follow the track along the cliff edge, do not go through the gate which has a 'No footpath' sign on it which appears in the fence in 100 metres or so, but continue up the hill in the direction of the footpath sign, keeping the fence on your left.

At the end of this path and to your left is a gate, proceed through this and then right past Nant-y-big farm and on down the road.

At this stage you will have been walking for about 1½ to 2 hours. Keep on this road until it meets up with a larger road, then turn left if you wish to link with the 'Trwyn Cilan loop', *(see page 59), if not, turn right and follow this road until you reach the crossroads in Sarn Bach. At the crossroads you will see on your left a house which used to be a blacksmith, next door was a shop. Note the old signpost standing at the crossroads.

Here a choice of routes is possible, either a simple return to Abersoch along the main road, or for those of you with some remaining energy, an interesting detour overlooking Hell's Mouth Bay, which returns to Abersoch via Llanengan: for this route turn left up the hill towards the Sarn Bach Junior school.

(If the following walk is taken in conjunction with the Abersoch-Porth Ceiriad walk, it will add approximately one hour.)

Turn left and through the gate in front of the school, if this is closed (usually to keep sheep in), use the top entrance which is 150 metres or so further on (Fferm Tŷ Newydd).

Proceed past farm buildings and then, after about 150 metres, arrive at the gate (please close). Take the left path after the gate and proceed down into the valley, turn right at the bottom of the hill in front of a field gate and walk along the path, keeping the rock face on your right. Follow this path over a series of

After leaving Porth Ceiriad, you will eventually descend onto a country lane which leads back to Abersoch

The old blacksmith's building, at the crossroads in Sarn Bach

stiles until you reach a farm. Above and on your right you will see the smelting chimney, some 50 feet high, go through the gate, and then, just past the farm cottage on the right will be seen the spoil heaps of old mine workings. Zinc was mined in this area as well as lead. Proceed along this path passing the Sun Inn on your left, this may be a welcome sight on a warm summer's day!

Head right when emerging onto the main road, and on your left is the east gate of Llanengan church (7), opposite the entrance to 'The Rock' restaurant.

On the left side of the road when leaving the village is an old water pump set in a wall with access steps in it, for the benefit of the cottages behind the wall.

The old mill (8) can be seen on your left on top of a hill, as you go up the hill out of the village, it is opposite to a graveyard – the chapel of which has been recently demolished. There is a footpath up to the mill and there are good views to be had from here, so it's well worth the effort.

As you carry on down the hill into Abersoch you will see in front of you a splendid view overlooking St Tudwal's Island East and the Rhinogydd mountains.

History notes
1. Abersoch golf links is an area of common land, comprising 25.3 hectares, it is under joint ownership between Mrs A. Jones, Abersoch, Mrs M. Jones, Abersoch and the Midland Bank Trust Co. Ltd. There are rights to graze 24 cattle and sheep to a grazing density of '8.9 sheep units per hectare'. (Fortunately for the greenkeepers these rights are not exercised: at present anyway!)

Within the golf course and to the right of the path you will see an extensive patch of dense low woodland, this is a marsh and fen area and is designated as a Nature Conservancy Council Site of Special Scientific Interest or SSSI for short. The interest in the area is botanical and ornithological. The old name for this area is 'Cors Lleferin' which means 'trickling marsh'.

2. Just to the right of this juncture are the remains of old lead mine workings, nothing of particular note remains at this spot. The track you are about to take however, is interesting as it was the bed of the railway track which was used to transport lead ore along to the point where the old lifeboat station now stands and this is where the ore was loaded aboard ships bound for Pwllheli, and from there to Cardiff and other places for smelting.

3. The southern shore of Llŷn had one great hazard for the Pwllheli shipping trade, Porth Neigwl (*Hell's Mouth*). This dangerous bay was however, offset by a

renowned safe anchorage, namely St Tudwal's Roads.

Lewis Morris in his survey of ports and harbours made these remarks in 1748:

St Tudwal's Road (Stidwells):

This is reckoned to be one of the best roads in Great Britain, it being a good Outlet and so Extensive, that it would contain the whole Royal Navy of England. On the South West Side of this Road there might be made a

The lighthouse on St Tudwal's

good dry Harbour, for small Vessels, by running out a Pier of Stones from Penrhyn Du Point to the Northwards.'

It was proposed to carry out the construction of a harbour in St Tudwal's Road in 1867 (probably in front of where the old lifeboat house is now, and inward to where the boat yard stands), as anticipated by Lewis Morris, but it was a pipe-dream and came to nothing.

4. These are the lead mines of Penrhyn Du and are of very ancient origin, they are normally associated with 19th century industrial history, but there is evidence of workings here which date from Roman and Phoenician times, indeed, it is said that an anchor stock was found on Porth Ceiriad beach of typical Phoenician design, there is also reputed to be a cliff-cave in the vicinity known as the 'Phoenician cave' which contains human skulls and other bones.

The Cornish mining pump-house at Penrhyn Du

A revealing letter written in 1668 by the agent of the landowner, Lord Herbert, Cherbury, reports that the 'best works' had been drowned out, but eighty tons of ore have been shipped and sold at £420, and more remains in the store house awaiting the ships' return. The whole of this £420, however, was needed to cover the cost of 18 months of wages for the workers and debts incurred on storage and various provisions for the workmen. This indicates the relatively small scale of the works at that particular time, despite the backing capital of a wealthy landlord.

In 1764, the whole of the mine workings were leased to the mining company, Roe of Macclesfield, who in 1782, introduced a Boulton & Watt steam engine to combat the continuous threat of flooding.

In 1870, a local miner, E. Lloyd Roberts, struck a rich ore pocket and sold rights for £5,200, soon after there were eight separate undertakings in the area, employing in the busiest period, around 200 men.

By 1880 'Slaters Directory' recorded three Abersoch based lead mining companies: the East Assheton Mining Co., the Tanybwlch Mining Co., and the West Assheton Mining Co. (Assheton was the name of the owner of the Vaynol estate which held extensive lands in Caernarfonshire. The estate was granted to John Smith the then speaker of the House of Commons. Thomas Assheton succeeded to the estate in 1774, and added the Smith family name to his own).

All this activity was relatively short-lived, for most workings had ceased operating by 1895.

5. Just in front of this and now commemorated by a plaque is 'Cornish Row', these cottages were so called because they were occupied by workers who were brought here from the Cornish tin mines on account of their experience in this kind of work, some of their descendants still live around here.

6. Although safe for bathers in calm weather, the ship *Franchise*, went aground off Porth Ceiriad in 1855, in thick fog.

7. Llanengan church – This church is the finest in Llŷn and is well worth a visit. It can be entered by the small lych gate in the road near the pub or through the main entrance in the west tower. The lych gate still incorporates some 16th century timber in its construction.

The church was founded by King Einion in the 7th century. Einion was the son of Cunedda Wledig, a Brythonic overlord who moved his family and his warriors from southern Scotland (as we know it today)

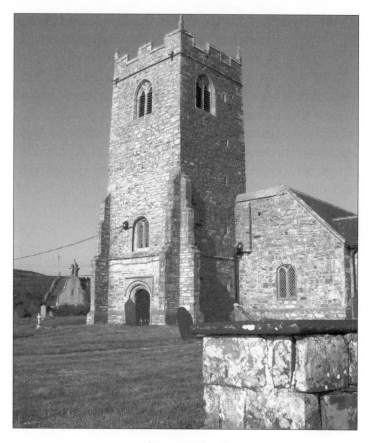

Llanengan church

to northern Wales after the Romans left Britain. Einion became the King of Llŷn and is buried at this church he founded at Llanengan.

The church has many features of architectural interest. It consists of a chancel and nave, and a south aisle of the same total length, there is a south porch and an imposing west tower.

The main construction is mostly of the late 15th century and the first third of the 16th century. The west tower was added in 1534, as dated by an inscription.

The church was a popular place of pilgrimage in the later Middle Ages.

The bells of the church are traditionally supposed to have come from the medieval chapel of St Mary on Ynys Enlli (*Bardsey Island*), however, one bears a date of 1624, and the other a date of 1664, which would obviously preclude them from existing in medieval times, it is possible that these dates refer to re-casting and not original working, so the tradition cannot be totally discounted.

Above the main west doorway of the west tower can be seen a long inscription in rustic Roman capitals.

8. The windmill, which is now ruinous, stands about 20 feet high. It is about 20 feet in diameter at the base and tapers to about 15 feet at the top. This was obviously not the top of the original building, indeed there are beam-slots visible for a second floor. The rubble-built walls are about 2 feet thick and would have been externally plastered.

Selection of original walk, originally published in:
Walks in the Llŷn Peninsula
Part 1: South and West

by N. Burras and J. Stiff

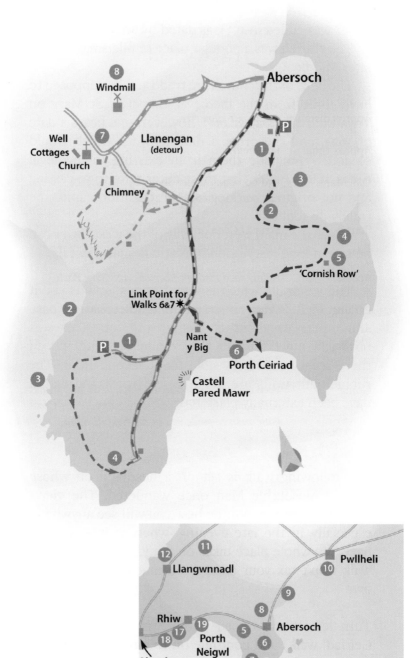

Walk 7
Trwyn Cilan

Walk details
Approx distance: *2 miles/3.2 kilometres*

Approx time:	*1-1½ hours*
O.S. Maps:	*1:50 000 Landranger Sheet 123* *1:25 000 Explorer Sheet 253*
Start:	*Mynydd Cilan car park.* *Grid Ref. SH 302 248*
Access:	*Follow road through Abersoch and Sarn Bach.*
Parking:	*Grassy car park on Mynydd Cilan common.*
Please note:	*Some areas of Mynydd Cilan have wet/marshy ground. This would be worse after heavy rainfall.*
Going:	*Very enjoyable walk because it follows an obvious path along Mynydd Cilan, with many 'Wales Coast Path' posts to guide you in the right direction.*

The following walk is set on a headland on whose surface Mesolithic Man once wandered. The views from here are some of the best you will see anywhere, especially in the late evening, when, if it is slightly hazy, the whole place takes on a mystical quality. The walk won't tax your energy too much if taken on its own.

Turn left at main road (from * in 'Abersoch-Porth Ceiriad' walk) and continue on this road, past an old

The grassy car park on Mynydd Cilan

Marshy ground on Mynydd Cilan

Follow this path to the edge – but not too close, for a spectacular view of Porth Neigwl (Hell's Mouth)

chapel on your right until you reach a right turn at a house called Erw Deg.

A hundred metres or so into the field opposite this turn off will be seen a mound. This is the remains of what is called a promontory fort, this is known as Castell Pared Mawr. It occupies a superb cliff-top position and was sited here, obviously from a defensive standpoint. It is pre-Roman in origin, from the Celtic Iron Age. It is only a small fort and would maybe have accommodated a similar number of people to Pen-y-gaer near Abersoch. It probably ceased to be occupied after the Roman period.

Proceed down this winding road until you pass over a cattle grid where you will turn left. If you are in a car there is parking on your left (1).

Look towards Porth Neigwl (*Hell's Mouth*) (2) and walk in that direction, turn left immediately after passing a very small house. Continue for 200 metres approximately, and then turn left.

Just as you reach the end of the wall, and if you wish, turn right and follow the gully to an interesting section of the cliffs at Trwyn y Ffosil (3).

Back on the main path and heading south, keep the field boundaries on your left and the sea on your right.

Keep on this track, passing in a little while a 'trig point' at Pen-y-mynydd. From this point carry on and in a couple of hundred metres you will see a grass-covered promontory on your right called Trwyn Carreg-y-tir, which juts out from the cliffs a little way, from there you will see some magnificent views of the Cilan cliffs.

Cross over into this field, where Porth Ceiriad is to be seen in the distance

When back on your track continue around the headland (4) until in a few hundred metres there is a definite cross track.

Take the left fork and follow this over the ridge in the near distance. You will shortly meet with a fence and a stone step stile, climb over this and head towards what looks like a small open gate, go through this and walk towards the farm, you will enter the beginnings of what looks like a funnel caused by two walls of a field coming together into a lane.

You are now coming into a farm called Cilan Uchaf farm and the track you are now on is not a footpath but is a courtesy path, so please take special care here to be as quiet and unobtrusive as possible, go through the gate and head straight through the farmyard to connect with the main road again.

Continue along this road back to Abersoch, if you came by car, follow it until you come to the road on the left called the Lôn Las with a house on the corner

The left-hand turning towards
Mynydd Cilan at Lôn Las

called Erw Deg and walk until you meet the cattle grid and your car, or, keep on the main road until you come to the crossroads at Sarn Bach where you can pick up the short detour through Llanengan, if desired.

History notes

1. Marked on many editions of the O.S. map is an antiquity called Castell Cilan, it lies just behind the small group of houses on the right as you face Hell's Mouth, it is now thought however, that it is only a natural mound.

2. Hell's Mouth or Porth Neigwl is a magnificent four mile strand, but it is not called Hell's Mouth without good reason, being one of the most treacherous tracts of coast in the whole of Wales. There have been literally hundreds of vessels which have been lost within its rocky jaws.

The name Porth Neigwl is a reference to one Nigel de Loryng or Lohareyn, who was granted extensive lands and estates in this area by the Black Prince, including Pwllheli and Nefyn. He had distinguished himself in the wars in Gascony, particularly at the battle of Poitiers.

Here is a quick selection from the long list of maritime wrecks which have been played out on this strand:

1824 – an Irish ship wrecked with a cargo of tobacco

Today's beach adventurers at Porth Neigwl

1839 – *Transit* with a cargo of cotton
1840 – *Arfestone* with a cargo of gold
1866 – Schooner *Henry Catherine*
1883 – Barque *Penseverenza*
1878   *Twelve Apostles*
1898 – Schooner *Idea* also schooner *Joseph Nicholson*

3. Fossil point is so named from the fossil trilobites (Cambrian/Ordovician arthropods) which have been found here, you will also notice some interesting stepped stratification of the cliffs.

4. The following are some notes on the land-use of this area:

The common land of Trwyn Cilan covers an area of 87.5 hectares in a single unit, there are grazing rights for 900 sheep, 79 cattle, 30 geese and 3 ponies, with a grazing density of 18.8 'sheep units' per hectare.

On Pen Cilan there has been found evidence of very early settlement by man. Microlith tools (very small stone flakes set together in a piece of wood to form saw-type blades etc) have been found here of a Mesolithic date. These people were hunters and have left no evidence of what their dwellings were like, in fact they might have been largely nomadic in their lifestyle and may have occupied this site only at intervals, probably during the summer. The central area of the headland is always wet, marshy and dotted with small ponds, it may have been the same in Mesolithic times and thus would have been a source of fresh water for dwellers in ancient times, as it has been, until the very recent past.

It is interesting to note that in these times the sea level was much lower than it is now, so that any dwellers on this headland were not, on the south and east at least, living on the sea's edge. From this headland if you look towards Porthmadog, a distance of some 15 miles, to where Sarn Badrig or St Patrick's Causeway juts out into the sea – Sarn Badrig, incidentally, was a danger to shipping perhaps second only in its notoriety to Hell's Mouth. All the bay north of a line roughly from the end of Sarn Badrig across to St Tudwal's Islands and Cilan Head was all dry land. Indeed, there is a legend concerning this Cantre'r Gwaelod (or the lowland hundred).

As recounted in the medieval manuscript of the Welsh 'Triads' Seithenyn was the keeper of the sluice gates in the sea wall, he became drunk one night and forgot to close the gates against the incoming tide and the sea covered Cantre'r Gwaelod, all the houses and land contained in it were lost. There were said to be sixteen fortified towns in the land 'superior to all the towns in Wales except Caerleon on the Usk'. Cantre'r Gwaelod was the land held by Gwyddno king of Cardigan. The people who survived the inundation escaped into the lands of Llŷn and Snowdonia.

These legendary events are placed in the 6th or 7th century AD.

Selection of original walk, originally published in:
Walks in the Llŷn Peninsula
Part 1: South and West

by N. Burras and J. Stiff

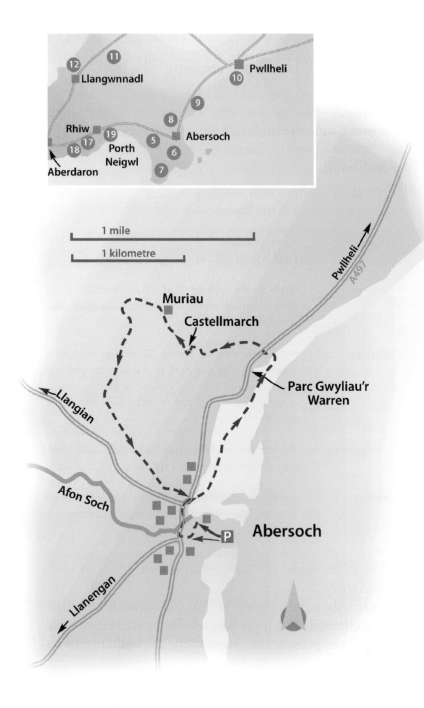

Walk 8
Castellmarch, Abersoch

Walk details
Approx distance: 4 miles/6.4 *kilometres*

Approx time: *2½ hours*

O.S. Maps: 1:50 000 *Landranger Sheet 123*
                1:25 000 *Explorer Sheet 253*

Start: *Abersoch beach*
                Grid Ref. SH 318 281

Access: *Walk to the lifeboat shed at the bottom of the harbour; turn right towards the harbour and boatyard.*

Parking: *Not many parking places. There are numerous restrictions. You can park in a public car park on the road towards the golf club, or by the community centre, but you must pay in both places during the season.*

Please note: *Not wet during the summer but the lane down from Muriau can get wet following a long period of rain.*

Going: *Great care should be taken when crossing the road between 'Warren' and 'Castellmarch' caravan park.*

The kidnapping of Castellmarch's master
The story
Near Abersoch there is an old mansion called Castellmarch, but there was a building there centuries before the present one. Here's how the building got its name:

Once, a king lived there, and he was called March ap Meirchion. March was one of King Arthur's knights. Despite being a wealthy man, he was unhappy. His ears were like horses'! He wore his hair long to hide them. The only one who knew of this was his barber, and he had promised not to tell a soul.

But March found it difficult to keep his secret, so he went down to the edge of the river Soch and whispered it to the water and the rushes that grew there.

Some months later, he held a grand feast at Castellmarch and Maelgwn Gwynedd the piper was asked to come to entertain everyone. On his way there, Maelgwn stopped at the river Soch and cut a reed to make himself a new pipe for the feast.

When the guests had all started to eat and drink, Maelgwn was asked to play his pipe. He blew hard. But instead of a beautiful melody, a voice came from it saying, 'March has long ears!' March and Maelgwn were shocked. March was a king, so everyone was afraid to laugh at his long ears, but he was very glad that everyone now knew his secret.

But March ap Meirchion was not the only extraordinary man to live at Castellmarch. During the 17th century, Sir William Jones lived there – he was friendly with a gang of smugglers who brought their goods ashore at the headland at Llanbedrog.

Sir William had a servant who was too enthusiastic and he'd had enough of him. He had tried to get rid of him several times, but the servant laughed it off every time, not believing that his master was being serious and refusing to leave the house. This servant had a strange influence on his master. Something had to be done; Sir William had had a bellyful of him. One night he went to visit the smuggler captain and told him

Castellmarch farm and holiday centre

about his problem. The captain gave him an idea. If Sir William paid him, the smugglers would come to Castellmarch in the dead of night, kidnap the servant, and take him with them to the south of France.

The plan was carried out, and they took the servant with them on their voyage. But the servant enjoyed himself so much that he decided to stay with the crew. Over time, he became a mate and, later on, captain of the ship!

One day he decided to return to Abersoch and play a trick on his former master. Sir William was invited to the ship for a feast before being shown all the wines the smugglers had to sell. But while Sir William was eating and drinking, the anchor was raised and the ship slipped out of Abersoch. Once again, the former servant held sway over his master.

The ship sailed with Sir William on board, and he saw many of the world's ports. In the end, after years

Your starting point is the beach at Abersoch

Be very careful when crossing this road from the Warren Caravan Park to Castellmarch Caravan Park

Looking down at Castellmarch farm

at sea, the servant forgave him and he was carried back to Castellmarch.

The walk

From Abersoch along the beach, over to Castellmarch and then back along the fields to Abersoch. This walk is best taken when the tide is out so that you can walk along the beach. To check the tide, visit www.pol.ac.uk/home/tides/ .

Park in Abersoch and walk to the crossroads in the village centre, or alight from the bus near the crossroads. Walk down the hill, over the bridge and right towards the harbour and boatyard on the right. You'll see a sign to the lifeboat on the right, follow it and pass the lifeboat building and on to the beach.

Turn left and walk along the beach. If the tide is in, this will not be possible unless you can go along the rocks. If so, the best thing to do is go back to the main road by going up the sandy lane before reaching a white house. Then up the hill and then down, and when you're almost at the bottom you will see a path with wooden steps going to the right

A view of Llanbedrog mountain, up above Castellmarch farm

through the woods down to the beach. Proceed then along the sand.

As you walk along the beach you'll reach houses behind the dunes. Keep an eye out for a lane through these dunes. Go along it and it will bring you into the Warren Holiday Park. Don't worry, a Public Footpath runs through the park.

Follow this path inland, above Castellmarch

Go straight ahead through the holiday park and out to the main road. Cross with care, looking in both directions, and go over towards the entrance to Castellmarch, through the small gate and up the road to the mansion. Go to the right past the mansion, through the

This single track lane passes a cluster of houses

Your final part of the walk leads you down to Abersoch

farmyard, and up the track. Half way up you'll reach a crossroads; keep right.

Go through the gate and continue along the track past Fferm y Muriau. Go through the gate into the farmyard, through another gate and down the track to another gate. Go through it and on until you reach a gate at the bottom of the hill. This track from Muriau can be wet following prolonged rainfall.

Don't go through the gate, but turn left and follow the fence. At the end of the fence, go right and down the wooden steps and over a stile, over a small bridge and up the slope to the left to an old track. Go left along the lane that goes along the bottom of the slope until you reach a stile. Go over it and straight ahead, past a small lake on the right.

Proceed to another stile and go over it and onward through the field to a thicket of gorse and a small bridge, and then into another field. Cross this field to another gorse hedge and another small bridge. It can be wet here too after a spell of wet weather.

Go on towards more gorse and a stile. Go over it

You will be faced with the harbour where you started the walk

and up the wooden steps to the field and along the right side of the field until you reach a kissing gate. Go through it and down the steps to a track. Go left and you will come to the main road near the harbour. Cross the road carefully, looking in each direction. Then walk to the right along the pavement back towards the centre of Abersoch, to the car or bus.

Translation of original text from
Anturio yn Llŷn

by Dafydd Meirion

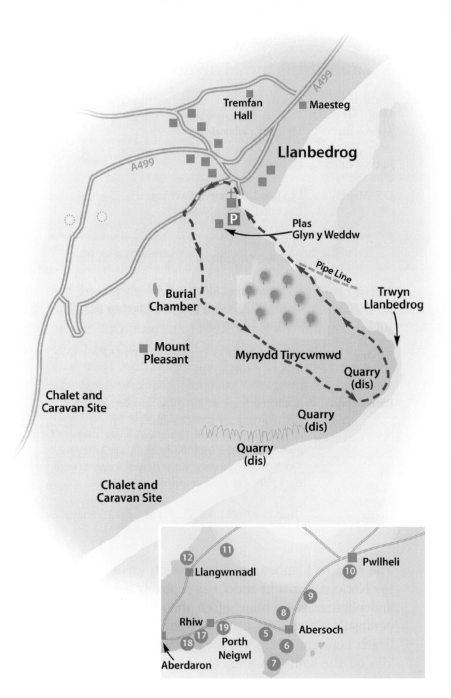

Walk 9
Llanbedrog and Mynydd Tirycwmwd

Walk details
Approx distance: 2½ *miles/4 kilometres*

Approx time:	*1½ hours*
O.S. Maps:	*1:50 000 Landranger Sheet 123*
	1:25 000 Explorer Sheet 253
Start:	*Llanbedrog*
	Grid Ref. SH 329 335
Access:	*Go towards the Church Hall from the car park, then up the hill following the second sign on the left for 'Mynydd Tirycwmwd'.*
Parking:	*National Trust or Oriel Glyn y Weddw car park. There is a parking fee.*
Please note:	*A narrow track with a lot of heather on it and a steep track on the eastern side of the hill.*
	Steps from Iron Man to the beach are steep and uneven, and even with the hadrails, can be slippery. The beach can be quite wet at times but easy to walk. High tides may prevent walking on the beach.
Going:	*Quiet lane from Llanbedrog to Mynydd Tirycwmwd.*

The road to Llanbedrog beach, which was bought by the National Trust in 2000, has probably been painted and photographed more often than any area on the peninsula. Ships used to unload coal and lime on the beach here and there are the remains of an old lime kiln on the southern end. The remains on the beach

The beach and Llanbedrog bay

was the slate carrying ship John and Margaret which caught fire in 1912 whilst waiting for fair weather to sail. During the English Civil War, Cromwell's army used St Pedrog's church as a stable. Walls and gravestones were broken as well as an ancient window on the eastern side. The pieces were later kept in a large chest, and when the present church was built in 1865, they were used to form a window on the west side.

The walk – from Traeth Llanbedrog, past Plas Glyn y Weddw, to the top of Mynydd Tirycwmwd and back.

Park your car in the National Trust car park by the beach or Plas Glyn y Weddw car park by the gallery. If coming by bus, disembark in the village and follow the signs to Plas Glyn y Weddw and beach, and start your walk from the entrance to the gallery. Otherwise go out of the National Trust car park entrance and go to the right, past the entrance to Oriel Plas Glyn y Weddw, a shop and St Pedrog's church – all on the left – and to a junction. Here, go to the left and before reaching the Church Hall, go left again and up the hill and to the right.

Ignore the footpath to the left and continue up the hill and through the trees. You will now come across

another footpath on your left, pointing to Mynydd Tirycwmwd. Follow the track to a junction and go to the right up the slope. Ignore the stile on the left and go straight ahead, through a gate, under an arch of trees and to a farmhouse and go straight ahead up the path, through the gate, through the trees and up the steps.

Ignore the path on the left and go straight ahead. Behind you is a magnificent view of the Eifl peaks and Llanbedrog and to the left the Llŷn coast and Pwllheli. Ignore the track on the right and go left. Near a large circular pile of stones go to the right to the trig point on the summit of Mynydd Tirycwmwd. In front of you are Abersoch, St Tudwal's Islands and St Tudwal's Roads. If you followed the path straight ahead of

St Pedrog's church, Llanbedrog

77

A cairn on Mynydd Tirycwmwd

The path meanders through gorse and heather

The viewpoint naming the mountain peaks at the summit

you, you would reach Abersoch.

After a rest, turn to the left and return to the pile of stones and a viewpoint naming the mountains of Gwynedd to the east. Go right and keep to the right. Continue straight ahead, ignoring the paths to the left and right. Follow the path down to the left, ignore the narrow path to the right and go straight ahead to the Iron Man sculpture. Should you find yourself on one of the smaller paths veering to your right, carry on and eventually the path will be bring you to the Iron Man.

Go to the right and down the steps until you reach the beach. During an unusually high tide, it may not be possible for you to get onto the beach here, therefore you should ask locally before you start this walk in winter.

Go to the left, past the Boathouse, and then up the path and to the right. At the junction, go to the right and down past the cottage on the left and to the beach. Go over the stream, to the left and up the hill past the cafe and toilets and back to the car park.

Other Points of Interest
Abersoch – between 1774 and 1854, 14 ships were built in the harbour here, and coal ships used to unload their cargo on the beach. Abersoch developed as a tourist destination during the second half of the 20th century, due mainly to the excellent sailing in Bae Ceredigion.

Mynydd Tirycwmwd There were three quarries here at one time, producing chippings and setts or paving stones, and a pier (parts of which remain), was built on the beach to export them. Here also is Ogof Wil Puw, a cave in which a local pirate kept his treasure.

Oriel Glyn y Weddw

Oriel Glyn y Weddw – was built for Lady Love Jones Parry as a dower house in 1856. She never lived here, but visited it occasionally. In 1896 it was bought by Solomon Andrews, a Cardiff businessman. The house was converted into an art gallery which housed paintings by Gainsborough and Turner and the stableyard was roofed over to form a ballroom which was also used for afternoon teas. Visitors used to arrive by tram from Pwllheli and was one of the main attractions of the area. The property was sold in 1946 and then fell into disrepair until it was bought by

*The Iron Man of Mynydd
Tirycwmwd*

Dafydd and Gwyneth ap Tomos who restored the building and opened it again as an art gallery. The house is now owned by a trust and has recently added a good café, an open-air amphitheatre and a woodland walk to its attractions.

Iron Man sculpture The original sculpture was a tin man, a figurehead from a ship placed there by Solomon Andrews, owner of nearby Plas Glyn y Weddw. When it was burnt, the village decided to replace it with another one, which was commissioned for £7,000. It was placed in position in 1981, and became known as the Iron Man. However, this was also vandalised so that all that remained were the boots. Again the village decided to replace it, but this time using local village talent. It was placed in position by a helicopter on 1 June, 2002. This latest one is hollow and on a windy day the wind makes the Iron Man sing!

St Tudwal's Roads – used to be a safe anchorage for the numerous ships plying their trade along the shores, although a number of sailing vessels did meet an untimely end here. At one time there were plans to build a breakwater from Penrhyn Du to provide extra anchorages and to protect the ships loading ore from the mines but they did not come to fruition.

Ynysoedd Tudwal – are two islands; Ynys Fach is the one nearest the shore and it is said that at one time during a low tide it was possible to walk to it. In 1877 a lighthouse was established here with a white light flashing every twenty seconds and a red light which is seen from the Pwllheli end. The other is Ynys Fawr; it is said that Saint Tudwal lived here at one time and there are the remains of

Abersoch and Cilan from Mynydd Tirycwmwd

monastic settlements of different periods here. The last monk was Father Henry Bailey Maria Hughes but he had to leave the island in 1887 when a great storm destroyed his monastery. In the middle if the 20th century, there were plans to establish a nudist colony here but nothing came of them. A few years ago, most of the animals living here died. There used to be Soya sheep here who lived on seaweed, deer and rabbits but the only animals now remaining are black rabbits. Shards of Roman pottery have been found during excavations on both islands. The larger island is owned by television scriptwriter Carla Lane, best known for the comedy series *Liver Birds*.

Originally published in
National Trust Walks 1. Northern Wales

by Dafydd Meirion

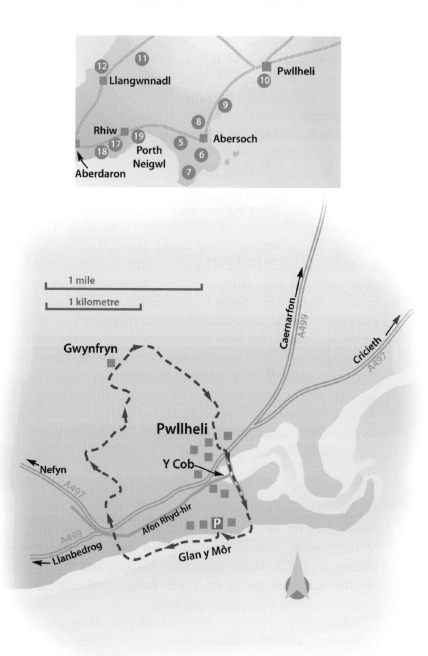

Walk 10
Pwllheli

Walk details
Approx distance: *3½ miles/5.6 kilometres*

Approx time: *1½ hours*

O.S. Maps: *1:50 000 Landranger Sheet 123*
                      1:25 000 Explorer Sheet 253

Start: *Glan y Môr (South Beach), Pwllheli.*
                      Grid Ref. SH 375 343

Access: *Walk westwards along the beach or the prom.*

Parking: *Plenty of parking places at the roadside.*

Please note: *Easy walk, no high slopes. The last part has a grass path, before joining the main road.*

Going: *Three quarters of the walk is safe with a path, but at one stage you have to cross a very busy road and great care is needed (A499).*

The story

There was great suspense amongst the children of the Peris valley on Saturday, 1 July, 1899. That was the day of the Sunday School trip, and that year they were visiting Pwllheli. There were 750 children and adults on the trip, all going by train from Llanberis to Caernarfon and then on to Pwllheli.

When they arrived, some visited the shops, but most, especially the children, went to the beach even though it wasn't a particularly fine day. As well as

South Beach – Traeth y De – Pwllheli

playing in the sand and swimming in the sea, boats could be hired for trips out on the bay.

And although it was rather windy with few showers, many of the children and adults wanted to go out to sea in one of these boats. One of those rowing the boats was Robert Thomas, a 19-year-old lad from Pwllheli. He'd just reached shore when he was told that there was another boat-load awaiting him – five children and four adults. They all embarked his boat.

Although the boat was full, three more children on the shore pleaded to join them, and Robert Thomas let them come along. The boat set off from South Beach and despite the rough sea the children enjoyed it. Robert Thomas was rowing at the bow of the boat, and most of the passengers were in the stern, and because of the weight, the rear of the boat sat low in the water.

The boat was nearly a mile out to sea when Robert Thomas realised that the wind had changed direction from west to south and so he decided to head back to shore.

But, as he turned, high waves struck the boat and threw everyone off balance. Because the boat's stern was so low in the water, the boat took on some water. One of the children shouted 'Dad, the water is coming into the boat.' Without thinking, the father tried to get to the stern and to his child. Robert Thomas called to him to sit down so that he wouldn't rock the boat, but as the father went to the stern, more water came in and everyone was scared. They all tried to move to the front, but by doing so the boat capsized and threw them all into the water.

Everyone was trapped under the boat, but Robert Thomas succeeded in pushing it up to free them from underneath it. But, aside from him, no one could swim. They were splashing and screaming in the water.

Robert Thomas caught hold of a little girl called Elen and tried to save her from drowning, but the weight of her clothes and boots made this an impossible task and she sank under the waves.

By now the waves had pushed the boat away from them, but another boat had seen what was happening and had rowed frantically towards them. Robert Thomas was dragged, unconscious, to William Peters' boat but there was no hope of saving anyone else. They lay motionless in the sea.

William Peters decided to row as fast as he could to the shore to get help. Two boats went back out with him and they succeeded in lifting four of the bodies into the boats and getting them back to land. But days went by before the other bodies were found.

Everyone was deeply saddened on the train back to the Peris valley that night. Twelve had lost their lives in

From the sand dunes, follow this footpath inland

You are now leaving the edge of the golf course, and heading in another direction through this kissing gate

This tunnel of trees runs beside the golf course

the tragedy – nine children and three adults.

The walk
From Pwllheli beach, towards Efailnewydd and back to Pwllheli.

Park the car at South Beach, Pwllheli. If you come by bus, you will alight on Y Maes and should walk towards the railway station and then along the Cob towards South Beach. On South Beach, walk to the right towards Llanbedrog, either along the beach or along the prom and then along the path that goes past the dunes. Look out to sea and you will see where the twelve drowned.

You will go past a row of tall houses, then smaller ones, mainly bungalows. When you reach the last house but one, you will see a path sign directing you to the right. Go down the track towards a large kissing gate and then along a path through woods that

Pont Llechan crossing Afon Cymerau

goes past the golf course.

When you come to a fork in the path, in the rushes, go left. Then left again and over the slated bridge – Pont Llechan – that crosses Afon Cymerau. You'll emerge at the main road near a roundabout. Cross the road carefully and go along the path that runs alongside the road going to Nefyn. This is a safe path with a wall between it and the main road.

Proceed until you reach a Public Footpath sign and go through the gate on the left and follow the path past the

Afon Cymerau can be high-level during heavy rainfall

This footway is very safe, as there is a wall to separate you from oncoming traffic

This kissing gate descends from the main road, and goes in-land

This gate leads to farmland, which will eventually lead you back to Pwllheli

trees. Near a stone building, go left, following the path through a tunnel of trees and straight up past a sign bearing an arrow until you reach a gate. Go through it and straight ahead alongside the fence to another gate and then out to the road.

Turn left and down the road until you reach the entrance of a large white house called Felin-fach and a Public Footpath sign. Go down the lane towards the house, go past it and onwards until you come to a track. Go up the track, following it left towards a gate. Go through it and along the edge of the field to a wooden stile and to another track.

There, go straight ahead towards a gate. Go through it and to the right, to Gwynfryn's farmyard and holiday cottages. Follow the tarmac lane until you get to a road, then turn right. Walk along the right-hand side of the road and watch out for vehicles, even though it's a fairly quiet road. Proceed past Coleg Menai and down to Pwllheli, arriving at Salem chapel.

Go straight down Gaol Street and towards Y Maes, where there are plenty of cafes where you can get a drink or a bite to eat. If you have come by bus, this is where to catch your return bus. Keep left and go towards the railway station, then right and along the Cob back towards the beach. When you reach the prom, turn right and back to your car.

Ffynnon Felin Fach

This rusty gate leads you onto a grassy path, away from the main road and footway

Translation of original text from *Anturio yn Llŷn*

by Dafydd Meirion

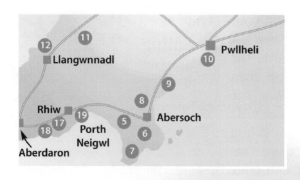

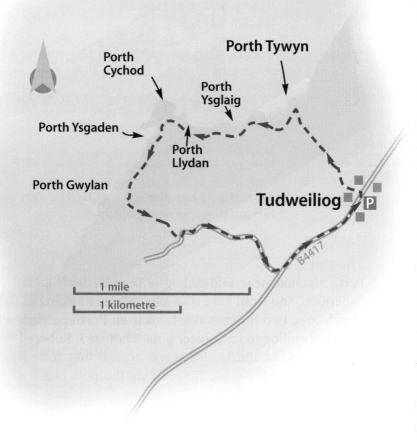

Walk 11
Tudweiliog

Walk details
Approx distance: *4½ miles/7.2 kilometres*

Approx time: *2¼ hours*

O.S. Maps: *1:50 000 Landranger Sheet 123*
                 1:25 000 Explorer Sheet 253

Start: *By the toilets (outskirts of the village Nefyn side).*
                 B4417 from Nefyn to Tudweiliog
                 Grid Ref. SH 239 371

Access: *Cross the B4417 towards the 'Ty'n Llan' caravan*
                 park.

Parking: *By the toilets, or anywhere at the roadside in the*
                 village.

Please note: *Narrow coastal path. No steep slopes to climb.*
                 Farmland suitable for walking.

Going: *The road at the beginning and the end of the walk is*
                 busy and there is no pavement/footpath.

The story
Porth Cychod near Tudweiliog is popular with local fishermen, and from here on a Wednesday morning in March 1933, two fishermen set out from Porth Sgadan near Tudweiliog to lay lobster pots. Thomas J. Roberts was 15 years old and Jac Jones was 25, and they rowed out on the sea for some time, laying the pots one by one.

Porth Sgadan

But suddenly they lost one of their oars. They couldn't row properly with the remaining oar and the boat was swept further out to sea by the wind and tide. In no time at all, the Llŷn coast disappeared and they could see nothing but sea. It grew dark and there was nothing to be done but hold on tightly to the sides of the boat and hope that the wind or the tide would carry them back to Llŷn.

When morning came, there was no sign of land, and both of them were hungry and thirsty. Later, they saw a ship on the horizon. It was the Holyhead ferry. They tried to get its attention but it was getting dark and the ferry passed without seeing them.

The wind had risen by now and the waves were washing over the boat, and it took on water. Jac Jones used his hat to bail the water out. But suddenly, in the darkness, they saw land and fortunately the wind was carrying them towards it. As they neared the shore, the boat capsized and threw them both into the water, but they managed to swim ashore.

Had they reached Llŷn? No, they were in Kilkeel, on the coast of Ireland! They had been at sea for 35 hours! They walked from the beach to nearby houses and were given a warm welcome. One of the residents telephoned the Tudweiliog post office and the postmaster Mr D. Griffith visited their families with the good news that they were safe.

The Irish were kind to them both. They were given money for the ferry home, food and gifts and cigarettes! They received offers to buy their boat, but they both decided to keep it as a memento of their adventure. The Irish authorities paid to have the boat carried back to Tudweiliog on the Holyhead ferry.

They returned by ferry and then by train to Pwllheli and they were given a very warm welcome when they reached the railway station on the Saturday. There was a large crowd there, and also one in Tudweiliog as they arrived on the bus.

They were very lucky that they had a good boat. That very same boat had been used to carry people over the perilous strait to Bardsey Island. And they were lucky too that the wind had carried them to Ireland, for if it had blown southwards, they would have reached the Atlantic and maybe even America!

The walk
From Tudweiliog to Porth Towyn, along the coast past Porth Cychod to Porth Gwylan and back to Tudweiliog Park your car near the toilets in Tudweiliog or, if coming by bus, there is a bus stop a little further up near the post office. Go up the hill until you see a Public Footpath sign and the Ty'n Llan Caravan Park

Enter this open land, which descends down to the beach

A quiet cove beach, to be seen from the coastal path

Take the left turning up the slope

Looking out towards the sea

on the right, or, if you came by bus, go down the hill and the signs are on your left.

Proceed along the track until you reach a caravan park and you will see a kissing gate on your right. Go through it and follow the left side of the field to a gate, and a kissing gate. Go through it and along the edge of another field until you reach a large gate and a small gate. Go through the small gate and along the track to another gate. Go through it and onwards past a farm to a small road.

Cross the road and you will see a gate ahead of you and a Public Footpath sign. Go through the gate and straight ahead along the field towards the sea, keeping the caravans to your left. You will come to a sign. You have a choice here. Either go down the lower path to the sandy beach of Porth Towyn and walk along to the far end of the beach and then climb the steep slope to the coast path. Or follow the higher

Looking back at the beach at Towyn, Tudweiliog

path that takes you past the caravans until you reach a gate and some steps. Don't go up the steps, but follow the path to the right that follows the bank.

You'll reach a stile. Go over it and follow the path along the fence to down to a stile and over a bridge towards caravans at Porth Ysglaig. Here are remains from an old mill and Ffynnon Cwyfan (*ffynnon*: well; Cwyfan: 7th century saint), and it is said that warts will heal if pins are dropped into the water there. Near Porth Ysglaig, in 1867, a ship foundered during its voyage from Spain to Liverpool carrying a load of nuts for Christmas.

Continue to a Public Footpath sign and follow the path up the slope until you reach Porth Llydan near a kissing gate. Go through it and follow the path up the steps and along the fence. Up the steps and keep right along the edge of the bank to an OS trig point. Beneath you is Porth Cychod and its corrugated iron huts for

The path runs between the fields and the sea

Yet another cove beach, tucked away from the main beach

storing fishing gear. This is where the two in the story (above) set off for Ireland.

Continue onwards, and with a chimney on your right you will reach Porth Ysgaden. Here there is an old kiln (where local women used to come and knit in its fire's warmth). This was a very busy place in the 18th and 19th centuries as ships from Ireland, Liverpool and Chester came carrying crockery, iron, leather, tobacco, tea, coffee, wine, sugar, oranges and coal, and the old coal yards can be seen once you get past the kiln.

Go past the old coal yards and through a kissing gate until you reach a gully and another kissing gate. Go through it and onwards to Porth Gwylan. This is as far as this walk goes along the coast. How about stopping here for a picnic? Then go to the sign and over the stile and follow the track to Porth Gwylan farm. Go through the farmyard and along the lane until you reach a junction. Turn left and although there is not much traffic, walk on the right-hand side facing oncoming traffic.

Keep going until you reach another junction and

keep right, passing Tyddyn Mawr farm on the left. At the next junction, keep right again and onwards until you reach the main road.

Turn left here, and once again walk facing oncoming traffic. You can walk along the grass for most of the way until you are back in Tudweiliog.

Porth Sgadan

Translation of original text from
Anturio yn Llŷn

by Dafydd Meirion

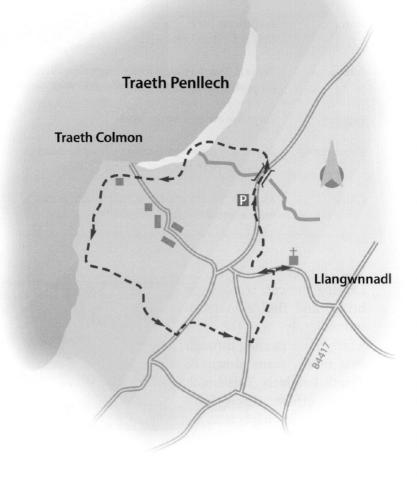

Walk 12
Traeth Penllech

Walk details
Approx distance: *4 miles/6.4 kilometres*

Approx time: *2¾ hours*

O.S. Maps: *1:50 000 Landranger Sheet 123*
                1:25 000 Explorer Sheet 253

Start: *Penllech car park*
                Grid Ref. SH 206 342

Access: *Towards Traeth Penllech along a narrow road. Free*
                car parking on the right-hand side of the road.

Parking: *Large free car park by the beach.*

Please note: *Steps and a steep slope leading up from the beach to*
                the coastal path. Wet land at Porth Tŷ Mawr.

Going: *Moderate on the coastal section; rough inland –*
                boots essential.

Walk directions
Leaving the car, recross the bridge and find a footpath immediately on the left which, after passing through two fields, leads down to Traeth Penllech. This beach is in effect three bays separated at high tide by rocky outcrops but

The footpath to Traeth Penllech

Traeth Penllech

becoming a mile long expanse of golden sand at low. At high tide it may be necessary to keep to the cliff top but along the shore is preferable. After wading across a shallow brook at the end of the second bay, you reach the third bay – but if the sea makes it impossible to get round the rocks, then there are steps up the cliff to the path above. Otherwise we continue to the far end of the beach where there is a slipway and boathouse. Going through the gate and up the steps we find that some thoughtful person has placed a welcome seat at the top which commands a magnificent view back along the bay. ¼ mile further on we drop down to the fishing cove of Porth Colmon.

Crossing the cove pick up the cliff path through a kissing gate to the right of the stone house and up some steps. Here we have a wide grassy headland above a rocky shore with numerous secluded coves and a brilliantly clear sea. A mile after leaving Porth

Porth Colmon

Colmon you come to the first steepish gully. Here the main route crosses over a stile in the bottom but we keep to the high side and follow it inland, then turn immediately left into a narrow sunken, very wet and overgrown lane. Over stile and bearing left, follow this lane, now becoming wider, then right, then through the gate to another field. Keep to the left side, then through a kissing gate and straight on until you reach an old deserted house. Turn left here up the farm lane to finally emerge on the road about twenty minutes after leaving the coast.

Turn left on the road and, in ¼ mile just past a corrugated iron shed, turn right at the footpath sign and immediately left through a narrow metal gate onto a raised, narrow, hedge-lined path. The path becomes severely overgrown at the far end but press on and look for a small wooden gate which leads down to the field on the right. Cross to the white cottage and the

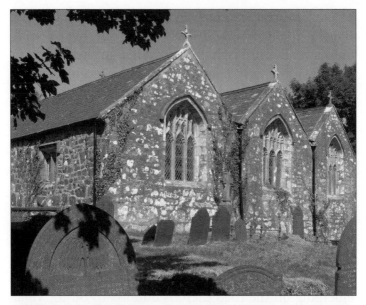

Llangwnnadl church

path actually goes through two gates in the back yard.
Cross the stream and go through the gate in front into

a field. Go straight across to a stile and keeping to the right of this very muddy field come out, over a stile, onto a road. Turn right and 50 yards up the road turn left down the farm lane to Ty'n Rhos. Passing straight through the farmyard go through the gate in front and keeping to the hedge on the right take the left of the two gates across the field. Again keeping the hedge on the right find a well-hidden wooden stile in the corner. Mid way along the far side of this next field is another well-hidden stile leading into a rough field. Now keeping the hedge on the left drop down to a stile in the corner out onto a road.

The pretty old pilgrim's church of Llangwnnadl set in the wooded valley just 50 yards to the right is well worth a quick visit. However, turning left after emerging on the road there is a footpath on the right by the old village school some 50 yards away. Through the kissing gate in the school grounds bear half left up to a stile in the far corner. Keeping to the top of this very rough field and without any distinct path through the bracken, gorse and brambles, find a very well-hidden stile in the far top corner which leads onto a proper field. Bear left to a stile across the field out onto the road. Turning right the car park is ½ mile down the road.

Originally published in
Llŷn Peninsula Coastal Walks

by Richard A. R. Quine

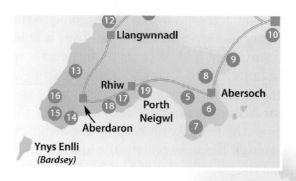

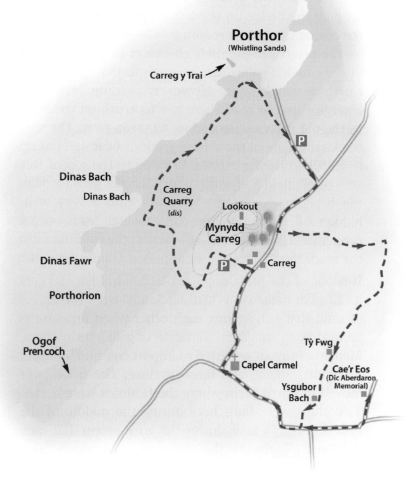

Walk 13
Porthor

Walk details

Approx distance: *4 miles/6.4 kilometres*

Approx time:	*1½ hours*
O.S. Maps:	*1:50 000 Landranger Sheet 123* *1:25 000 Explorer Sheet 253*
Start:	*Porthor, on B4413 from Botwnnog to Aberdaron.* *Grid Ref. SH 166 296*
Access:	*Turn right after Penygroeslon village towards* *Porthor.*
Parking:	*A pay and display car park near the beach.*
Please note:	*Wet land near Porthorion.* *High cliff path from Porthorion back towards* *Porthor.*
Going:	*Quiet footpath.*

It is one of the most popular beaches in Llŷn and gets its English name of 'Whistling Sands' from the grains of sand that rub against each other when pressure is applied such as when someone is walking on them. Many years ago it was used to import coal and lime and to export herring and farm produce. The trade later moved to Porth Ferin where the facilities were better. Two ships were built here during the middle of the 19th century. In 1859, during the great storm that sank the *Royal Charter* off the east coast of Anglesey, nine ships came here to shelter. Two ship were wrecked here in 1879 – the *Sellar* and the *Weaver*. In 1977, the schoolmaster of Aberdaron school was drowned here while trying to rescue one of his pupils, who also drowned.

The walk – Inland from Porthor and then back to the shore near Porthorion and back to Porthor.

The turning for the track

Park your car in the National Trust car park at Porthor (there is no bus service here), then walk back up the road and not to the beach. When you reach the junction, turn right and walk along the road until you reach a small forest on your right on the slopes of Mynydd Carreg. To the left is a Public Footpath sign, follow it down a narrow track until you come to a 'Private' sign. There is a kissing gate under an arch to your right. Go through it and across the field to another kissing gate and on to another one and another one until you come to a small wooden bridge and stile. Cross them and up the field until you come to a gate near caravans.

Dic Aberdaron's memorial

Go through the gate and past Tŷ Fwg and Ysgubor Bach until you come to a crossroads. You can either turn left and then straight ahead, not following the road to the right, to visit the plaque noting where Dic Aberdaron used to live and then return to the crossroads, or turn right and walk along the road until you come to Plasyffordd. Follow the

To the car park at Carreg

road to the right until you reach a sign for a National Trust car park at Carreg. Go left up a track to the car park, passing through a kissing gate to Mynydd Carreg. Turn left, following a tractor track which runs clockwise around a small hill until you are on the coastal side of Mynydd Carreg.

Follow the track until you come to a large gate and a kissing gate. Go

The track on Mynydd Carreg

through the kissing gate and on to a path which runs between two fields until you reach another kissing gate. Turn right and follow the path back Porthor and then up the lane to the to the car park. Why not rest on Porthor beach? It has lovely sand and a cafe and shop during the summer season.

Towards the coastal path

The coastal path at Porthor

Porthor beach

Other Points of Interest

Dic Aberdaron was a noted linguist, speaking, it is said, 13 or 14 languages fluently and with some knowledge of another twenty. They included Latin, Greek, Hebrew, French, Russian, Italian and German – and of course Welsh and English. His father was a carpenter and fisherman and it was assumed that Dic would follow him, but he was more interested in books, and when caught reading would be thrashed by his father. When he was twenty years old, he'd had enough and left home, travelling as far as Liverpool and on a number of occasions as far as London. He would do odd jobs for vicars and men of learning and would receive books as payment. He would walk the country, followed by his numerous cats, in an old army coat with its pockets full of books and on his head either a top hat or a hat made of rabbit fur with its ears sticking up. He also had a French horn which he would blow on entering a town or village. He died in St Asaph, Denbighshire, in 1843 at the age of 63.

Porthor

Mynydd Carreg Jasper was once mined here and was exported to be used as building stone, in places such as St James's Palace in London.

The summer beach café at Porthor and the lane back to the car park

Originally published in
National Trust Walks 1. Northern Wales

by Dafydd Meirion

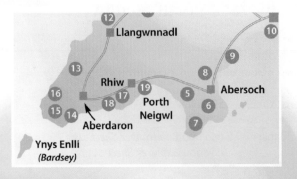

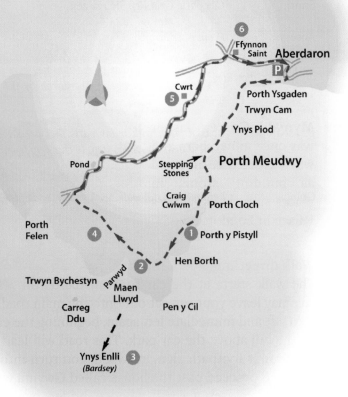

Walk 14
Porth Meudwy

Walk details
Approx distance: *4 miles/6.4 kilometres*

Approx time:　　*2½ hours*

O.S. Maps:　　*1:50 000 Landranger Sheet 123*
　　　　　　　1:25 000 Explorer Sheet 253

Start:　　　　*Car park. Grid Ref. SH 172 263*

Access:　　　*From Aberdaron.*

Parking:　　　*The National Trust car park (non-members pay) –
　　　　　　　at centre of the village of Aberdaron by the small
　　　　　　　bridge.*

Please note:　*Coastal path, with many parts that are steep and
　　　　　　　without defences. Steep steps to climb up from Porth
　　　　　　　Meudwy.*

Going:　　　　*Leisurely coastal walk, with grassy, wide paths.*

Walk directions
The walk starts at the car park in Aberdaron, where
you may leave your car, set out onto the main road and
turn left and immediate left again, beginning the climb
up the hill above the car park. This road will lead you
to the first footpath sign, at which, you turn into the
path and proceed past the house called Gwynfa where
the path crosses a small wooden bridge over Afon
Saint, in a few metres stop and take the short path on

Aberdaron

Go down this path, that leaves the road and takes you down towards the coastal path

Go over this footbridge

your left which overlooks the waterfall.

Retrace your steps to the main path and continue, taking in the views of the beach as you go.

This corner of the beach is called Porth y Simdde. Remains can be seen of an old building at the mouth of Afon Saint. This was probably a corn grinding mill. Remains can also be seen of an old jetty running into the sea.

In a couple of hundred metres or so you will notice a small promontory in the cliff this is called Trwyn Cam.

At the fork in the path take the top one as the other goes down to the beach, continue along this path until after a while you will pass through a kissing gate, if at this point you look towards the sea you will notice a large detached rock, this is called Ynys Piod. The path leads through another kissing gate and down some steps on to Porth Meudwy.

Porth Meudwy, a small fishing port, was an embarkation point for the

Looking back towards Aberdaron's shoreline

This kissing gate will lead you down to Porth Meudwy

Porth Meudwy fishing haven

These steps lead up from Porth Meudwy

Follow the path that leads around this very dangerous high cliff

pilgrims wishing to go to Ynys Enlli (*Bardsey*). It still has a timeless quality about it as you shuffle between the lobster pots and the fishing boats to get to the small stream opposite the path you have just descended. Cross the wooden bridge and make your way up the steep slope in front of you and through the kissing gate (at this point you can cut off from the path and take the other signposted track back to the road).

Carry along this path in the direction of Porth Cloch where you will take the new and slightly higher path: the old path which was much the more exciting one, is unfortunately now dangerous.

Keep to this track and cross over Craig Cwlwm. (Again, at this juncture there is a path to the Aberdaron road.)

Head along this path passing Porth y Pistyll (1).

In a while you will come to Hen Borth, keep to the path, and pass through 4 kissing gates, until you come to a crop of large rock. At this point you will be further repaid for all this walking by superb vista's across Bardsey Sound to the island itself, where, depending on the weather, it will be showing one of its many moods (3).

In the foreground is the attendant small island of

Carreg Ddu, a barren rock, and a resting place for seals and sea-birds. Beyond this, in the distance, is the barely discernible rocks of Maen Bugail. Directly in front of you is the cove of Parwyd.(2).

The memorial plaque at Bychestyn

After you have taken in the atmosphere of this very special place, head upwards towards the stone 'walkers' cairn at the summit of Pen y Cil (headland in the corner) where you will take the safe route to the National Trust property of Bychestyn (4).

Head towards the kissing gate inland, and cross this, heading left to the gates and through onto the headland.

Bychestyn land is owned by the National Trust

Walk along this path keeping the hedge to your right. Go through the kissing gate and turn right (sea on the left), heading towards Mynydd Mawr, until you are confronted by a fence, at this, turn right and walk along until you reach the end of the fence where you will take the left track through the gate. Head along this lane until in a short distance it meets with another slightly broader track where you will

Through these gates, you will be lead on to a single track road, and back to the car

bear right. Continue along this lane until you reach a pond Pwll Cyw, where the path splits left and right (the left path takes you up onto Mynydd Mawr). Take the path to your right and follow this small road to the farm called Cwrt, which is about half a mile distant (5).

After passing this farm, the second gate on your right is the entrance to Bryn Crocbren ('gallows hill').

Keep on this road until you meet with a T-junction where you will turn right and in a little while come to another T-junction where you will turn right again, bringing you onto the main road where you will shortly meet up with your car. At the last T-junction will be found Ffynnon Saint ('the saint's well') (6). The overgrown and barely visible well is positioned opposite the house of the National Trust warden about 10 metres into some undergrowth and is in a deplorable condition.

History notes

1. At Porth y Pistyll was discovered what is known as an 'industry of flint and stone', it was a location where man in the Neolithic period prepared tools for use in everyday life such as knives, scrapers, axes, arrowheads, fish-hooks etc.

2. The large cove in front of you is called Parwyd, which means 'partition'. At Parwyd in May 1959 and again in the April of 1961, on the top of the cliff which rises from the sea, were found five stone blades.

3. Ynys Enlli, known by the Vikings as Bardsey, has also been called 'The Rome of Britain' and 'The Iona of Wales'.

The origins of religious settlement on Bardsey go back deep into the Age of the Saints, and the

Ynys Enlli (Bardsey) from the sea

flourishing centuries of the early Celtic Church. It was certainly established as a refuge by AD 622 when the monks of Bangor Iscoed fled there to escape the Saxons. There may have been monks' cells on the island for at least a couple of centuries before this date. St Cadfan is the saint usually associated with the first religious foundation on Bardsey. Cadfan, with a large company of other 'saints' arrived in Wales from Brittany around AD 516 having been driven from his former territories by the Franks. Some of these other 'saints' established churches all over northern Wales and include the well-known Padarn as well as Gwyndaf and Hywyn (who established the church in Aberdaron). Over the centuries this monastic settlement became one of noted importance – the well-known legend of the 20,000 buried saints is a testimony to this importance in the eyes of the world, even if the figure is not literally correct it shows the measure of importance with which the island was held.

This remote religious sanctuary, before the Norman conquest, was constructed on very simple lines. The monks lived in separate 'cells' or huts which would have been wattle or stone built; there would have been a small church, a hospice and a cell for the Abbot, these were later built of timber and wattle. The whole was then enclosed by a wall, this arrangement was called a 'llan'. It is almost impossible for us today to comprehend the awesome simplicity and austerity of the life led by these monks in this remote, gale-swept, bleak and treeless island; they must have indeed felt that they were dwelling on the edge of the world.

Bardsey had always figured prominently as a place of pilgrimage. The pilgrims would have arrived in Llŷn from one of two directions:

The journey from the north, would be approached via Bangor, and having visited the Cathedral, he would make his way through the walled town of Caernarfon to Clynnog Fawr and the ancient church of St Beuno. He would then cross Yr Eifl and walk on through Pistyll towards Nefyn, and along the shore to Llangwnnadl and finally to Aberdaron.

If his journey brought him from the south, he would come through Pwllheli, arriving there perhaps by ship, and then on towards Llanengan via the church there. Then, on past Hell's Mouth and the climb towards Rhiw and on in the direction of the church of St Hywyn on the shore at Aberdaron.

4. There is evidence at Bychestyn of a farming settlement of possibly the 15th or 16th century. There are field boundaries in the area of gorse and heather between the present footpath and the cliff top.

Although there is not a lot to see due to this vegetation, aerial photographs show the marks clearly. The fields are divided up into strips or 'quillets', each strip being tended by one individual much in the way of the traditional medieval 'open field system'. These medieval-style holdings were still the norm in 1592, when a survey of the lands owned by the Abbey of Bardsey was carried out. Probably associated with these fields is a rectangular enclosure on Mynydd Bychestyn (a hill on the edge of the field system on the Aberdaron side), it measures 40 yards by 25 yards with remains of a hut about 15 feet square, which may have been clay or turf built.

5. 'Cwrt' as its name suggests, was once a court house. In fact it was the court for the manor of Bardsey. A manor in medieval and later times (up to late Tudor times when the 'manorial system' started to die out) was a holding of land over a wide area covering, sometimes, many parishes and villages.

6. Ffynnon Saint is a small 'D' shaped pool about 3 feet across surrounded by stone walling below water-level. It has an iron lid at ground level – not now visible. There is a 1 foot high dry stone wall surrounding the well on three sides leaving it open to the west.

Aberdaron tradition says that moles are never found on the Uwchmynydd side of Afon Saint!

Selection of original walk, originally published in:
Walks in the Llŷn Peninsula
Part 1: South and West

by N. Burras and J. Stiff

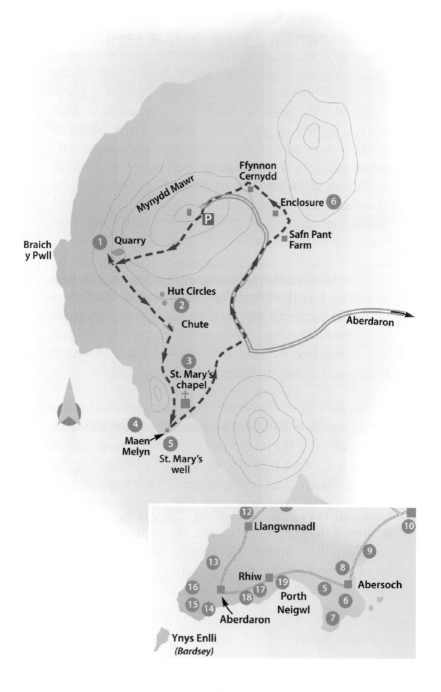

Walk 15
Mynydd Mawr – Capel Mair

Walk details
Approx distance: *2 miles/3.2 kilometres*

Approx time:	*1½ hours*
O.S. Maps:	*1:50 000 Landranger Sheet 123* *1:25 000 Explorer Sheet 253*
Start:	*Car park at Mynydd Mawr.* *Grid Ref. SH 140 258*
Access:	*B4413 from Aberdaron, up the hill towards Uwchmynydd. Continue on the road until you reach the top with Ynys Enlli (Bardsey Island) to be clearly seen.*
Parking:	*Car park for approx. 15 cars on the top.*
Please note:	*Steep climb with some dangerous places.* *The paths are rather narrow in places.*
Going:	*Rather a steep path leading to the car park at the top.*

Walk directions
Quite an easy walk with some fine views over Ynys Enlli and the surrounding area. If you have dogs with you, keep them under strict control here, as there are a lot of sheep about, and the gorse and heather tends to hide them until you are beside them.

The track from Mynydd Mawr

Start from the look-out point on the top of Mynydd Mawr, up which you can drive and park.

Look towards Ynys Enlli (Bardsey) and head in that direction onto a concrete path which will lead you down the hillside in its direction. There are fine views of the island and its monastery from here.

Continue down the path until you see some large and clearly defined quarry workings on your right (1). In a few metres you will come to a path which crosses yours, continue on over this until the next grass path where you will turn left. (Note – there are many possible grass paths to take, and they all lead to the same area.)

A short while after the quarry, you will come to a large outcrop of rock on your left, if you head up past this rock for a couple of hundred metres heading north-north-west, you will come to the remains of two hut circles on map ref: (SH 138 256) (2).

Retrace your steps to the path and in about 20 metres, keeping Bardsey on your right, you will see below you the remains of St Mary's chapel surrounded by low walls (3).

In the opposite direction to Aberdaron is a path leading off in the direction of the island. Make your way, **taking care down the rocks**, onto this path.

You will now be heading towards a rocky cove in front of you with the island on your right. As you pass a large outcrop of rock, turn towards Enlli and head in that direction to a standing stone called Maen Melyn ('yellow stone') on Trwyn Maen Melyn ('yellow stone point').(4).

With the island behind you, make your way to the rocky cove on your right where in a little while you will come to some stone steps, these lead down to Ffynnon Fair ('St Mary's well') (5), take care here if you wish to view the site.

After returning to the top of the steps, and with the island on your left, head towards Capel Mair ('St Mary's chapel').

The path above the waters of Swnt Enlli (Bardsey Sound)

Ynys Enlli (Bardsey) from Capel Mair

With the island behind you, head left around the hill in front of you and make your way towards the roadway at the top, keeping the island behind you all the way.

On emerging onto this tarmaced road, turn left and head uphill until the road swings sharply to the left, at this point you will leave the road and walk alongside the fence on a small footpath.

In a short distance the fence will drop away to your right but you continue along the path, noting that the fields in the distance towards the sea are long and narrow. These are known as quillets and are ancient field boundaries, more or less unchanged from the days when they were made.

Keeping this wall on your left follow the path along the wall. You are now heading towards Ffynnon Cernydd, in around a hundred metres you will see it set in a three-sided enclosure open to the east.

Set off now to return to your car on the top of Mynydd Mawr. Head up the hill behind the well until you meet the road, turn right and follow this to the end.

History notes

1. This rather scenically situated quarry is probably of the 19th century, the track which leads from its 'mouth' in the direction of Aberdaron was constructed by the quarry men for the transport of the quarry produce, there would have been a constant 'to-ing and fro-ing' of carts loaded with rock being pulled by men, mules or donkeys. There is an interesting feature to look out for where the track terminates on the edge of a rock bluff; if you look down to the foot of the bluff where the track, winding off to the left, is clearly visible you will see a well defined 'chute' in the rock face. This is where the carts would have been tipped at the top of the bluff and the contents tumbled down to the bottom to be reloaded on other carts for the next stage of the journey. The constant rolling of rocks down this steep slope has gouged out the 'chute' now visible.

2. These two hut circles, around 50 metres apart, are an indication of an isolated farming settlement. As has been previously stated in another walk, to accurately date these kind of remains is practically impossible as dwellings of this sort were the norm from the Celtic Iron Age period, through the centuries of the Roman occupation and well into the Dark Ages. The broad flattish area below them – on which the remains of St Mary's chapel now stands (referred to shortly), may have been an area cultivated by these remote-living

pastoralists – geographically and chronologically. This flattish area surprisingly, is often sheltered from the sea winds and it may not have been impossible for some hardy cereal crops to be grown here. It is also conceivable that animals such as sheep and goats, when not being allowed to roam free over the surrounding hills and mountains, could be corralled here in wattle or timber enclosures. A picture comes to mind when looking at a site like this of what a Dark Age 'farm' would have been like, an unbelievably austere existence by modern standards, yet all basic human requirements such as food, water and shelter would not necessarily have been in short supply. The dwellings occupied by these farming families are now represented by often poorly defined remains, such as those on this site. These were constructed by the erection of a rough stone wall vaguely circular, between ⅔ and 1 metre high, surrounding a sunken, beaten-earth floor. The roof would have been constructed in a 'teepee' fashion with long poles resting on the top of the stone wall rising up to an apex. The poles would have been covered over with either thatch, bracken, turf, or any combination thereof. There would have been a single entrance with a pole set in the ground at either side to support a leather door flap. The walls of the building would be draught proofed with mud and moss. In the summer, the hearth for cooking would be situated outside, but during the winter it would obviously be inside in the centre of the hut, the smoke would find its way out through holes and chinks in the roof. Inside there would be no 'furniture' of any kind, people would sit on the floor and beds were simply piles of straw or heather etc., on the floor. The fire would occupy the centre of the hut. Cooking and eating utensils would be simple and made of wood, wickerwork, leather or unfired clay. Hut circles such as these show much variation in size, between about 3 metres and 9 metres in diameter, no doubt the number of intended occupants would govern the size of the construction. A site such as this, with two small huts, would maybe represent the farming settlement of a single family.

3. The remains now visible, are of a building around 12 metres by 7 metres, surrounded by an enclosure roughly 84 square metres. The footings of this building have been dug out, some of the loose stones which would have been incorporated in the wall show signs of having been mortared. The enclosure, which surrounds the church remains, is a good example of an area of medieval cultivation. Indeed, William Williams (1738-1817) says: 'The plain in which it is situated is divided into a vast number of quillets (strips) which belong to as many different proprietors.' If indeed this plot of land was cultivated in the Dark Ages, possibly by the dwellers in the previously mentioned huts on the higher ground nearby, it would demonstrate a continuance of cultivation from the 5th, 6th and 7th centuries through the Middle Ages and probably into the 16th century and the Tudor period.

The earliest record of the remains as those of a church are of 1748. Interestingly, a late 18th century drawing shows the ruins of a typical 17th century house. However, it must be supposed that a church of some sort has been on this site since early medieval times at least. Exactly what it was like we do not know; one description states that it was 11 metres long by 4½ metres wide, not including the several dormitories that pertained to it. If this description is correct it is possible to visualise this as a small abbey which would have provided accommodation for pilgrims to Ynys Enlli (*Bardsey Island*). One can picture then, a small huddle of thatched stone buildings occupied by a few monks, possibly, largely self sufficient, growing a few crops on the surrounding cultivated enclosure, maybe with a few sheep on the adjacent hillsides.

4. This stone although leaning to one side is nevertheless a standing-stone, placed here by man in the Neolithic or Bronze Age.

Standing stones: what are they? what were they? Erected in Neolithic and Early Bronze Age times, enigmatic fingers of stone, placed seemingly at random over the whole of Britain, over Europe and with equivalents in many part of the world, but erected for what purpose? Archaeologists mostly suggest that they marked the sites of burials, indeed burials have been found under or close to some of them, but most, on excavation, have proved to be unconnected with any burials. So it would seem that this was not their function, what then was it? If you are equipped with a ruler or any other straight-edged implement and an Ordnance Survey map of virtually any area of Britain, and then locate the sites of all the standing stones marked on the map you will notice after only a few minutes work that you are able to line up many in various criss-crossing straight lines. Obviously, some of the alignments thus produced can be explained by chance, but usually, after a little diligence and perseverance with the map, very many more lines can be found than can be accounted for by chance. What you have found are examples of the controversial 'ley lines'. You may also notice that churches may appear in these alignments, indeed, any site which is demonstrably ancient i.e. prehistoric, will often be found to form straight lines with other such sites. It should be borne in mind that the vast majority, if not all old churches, are placed on pre-existing ancient pagan sacred sites. The policy of the Christian Church in its early years was not to try and establish new sacred sites, but to superimpose a Christian site onto an old pagan one, so that, in the eyes of the common people the old gods had been conquered and superseded by the new, whilst, at the same time continuing the sanctity of the site itself. It is for this reason that so many churches appear on ley lines. Other sites likely to appear on leys include stone circles, burial mounds, barrows, tumuli, dolmens, cromlechs and any other similar related or equivalent sites. Also included are some distinctive natural features, the most important being mountain tops, or particularly cairns on mountain tops.

This whole concept of ley lines was the 'rediscovery' of one Alfred Watkins in the 1920s. Watkins was an avid countryside rambler and walker and this version of the countryside laid out in a grid-like pattern reputedly came to him in a moment of inspiration. He published a book called *The Old Straight Track* and the cult of ley lines, as he called them was born. Needless to say, Watkins did not know what they were, nor do we today, although between his time and ours, rivers of ink have flowed carrying with them theories ranging from the banal to the bizarre. Some theories remain afloat, others sinking without trace, still others caught in eddies and backwaters, often to be flushed out again with a new flood of interest in the subject of ley lines.

The explanation offered by Watkins was that these lines were laid down in ancient times as way markers, route finders or trade routes etc. However, as interest in leys developed and more people began to investigate and plot them, and as the numbers found increased, it was shown that many lines passed straight through lakes, swamps, straight off cliffs and over inaccessible peaks, in short, direct but very inconvenient routes indeed. The way-marker theory has been almost totally abandoned. Modern theories of ley lines revolve around an idea that these lines are energy carriers of some sort, natural earth energy that manifests itself on the earth's surface in straight lines. In the past this energy, so goes the theory, was concentrated in various points by our ancestors, or did so naturally. Then marked by standing stones and such like where the accumulated energy could be used by certain individuals among the people, who were versed in the necessary techniques, for the benefit of the community e.g. helping the growth of crops or in healing the sick – indeed many stones today have folklore connected with them relating to healing. This whole concept is too esoteric for the acceptance of most archaelogists, the majority of whom do not even accept the existence of alignments in the first place.

Many sites on ley lines have associated folklore attached to them e.g. stones that move, stones that speak, stones that heal, buried treasure guarded by spirits, burial mounds guarded by serpents and dragons, all of which may be a garbled and distant folk memory of the 'treasure' of the energy which flowed along these lines. It is interesting to note that most people who practice the art of dowsing maintain that the lines are active today. The energy is still there,

The remains of Capel Mair

although the ley system is obviously much mutilated in present times with the destruction of so many ancient sites.

The authors have been able to ascertain that this stone, Maen Melyn, is the culmination (or start) of three ley lines.

5. In the rocks of the bay, beneath the site of the church, and covered at high tide, is the celebrated Ffynnon Fair. There is a folk-belief attached to this well. To quote Edmund Hyde-Hall:

> Below its site (St Mary's church) close upon the edge of the sea and only to be reached by descending a craggy and narrow path, dreadful to the sight and horrible to the imagination, is St Mary's Well, or Ffynnon Fair. The votaries who can bring to the chapel a mouthful of water,

Above Ffynnon Fair

unspilled and unswallowed, may be secure of their wishes' accomplishment; but it must be no ordinary object of cupidity or ambition which could tempt an inland-bred man to the experiment, however ardent his wish or strong his faith.

There is a slight variation on this legend which appears in an early 20th century guide book:

The other supposed object of special interest is Ffynnon Fair, 'Our Lady's Well', which occupies a hollow in the cliff a little to the right of the bottom of the rock staircase . . . and is only accessible at low tide. It is a little basin of freshwater filled by a tiny stream trickling down the rock and is about two feet deep. The pilgrim who was skillful enough to convey a palmful to the top of the cliff without spilling any had his fondest wishes granted. On the rock beside the well is the impression of 'Our Lady's' hand, also of the shoe of her horse.

Other slight variants on the legend state that the bearer of the water, on ascending to the church should then pass three times around it, also without spilling/swallowing a drop, before his wishes are granted.

6. This enclosure with its associated small building, possibly a house, may date from medieval times and represent another example of an agricultural settlement in this remote spot.

Selection of original walk, originally published in:
Walks in the Llŷn Peninsula
Part 1: South and West

by N. Burras and J. Stiff

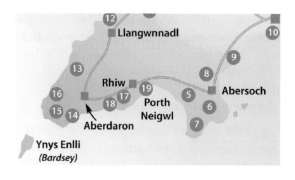

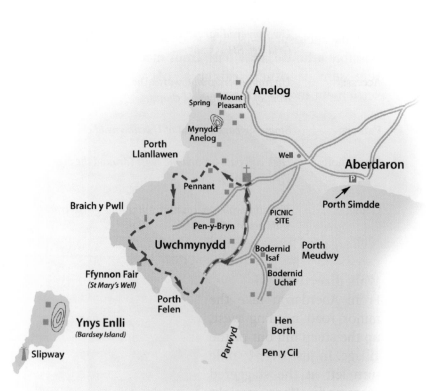

Walk 16
Uwchmynydd

Walk details
Approx distance: *2½ miles/4 kilometres*

Approx time: *2 hours*

O.S. Maps: *1:50 000 Landranger Sheet 123*
                 1:25 000 Explorer Sheet 253

Start: *Uwchmynydd car park*
                 Grid Ref. SH 155 265

Access: *Up from Aberdaron towards Uwchmynydd. Park in*
                 front of Uwchmynydd chapel.

Parking: *Stony car park in front of Uwchmynydd chapel.*

Please note: *High cliff path around the coast (around the area of*
                 Ffynnon Fair).

Going: *Pleasant walk on country lanes and grass tracks*
                 with superb views.

Walk directions
From Aberdaron take the minor road heading west, up the steep hill out of the village. In just over ½ mile turn left at the staggered crossroads. Keep straight ahead for ¾ mile, pass a chapel on the left and immediately after rounding a steep bend with a

Uwchmynydd chapel

135

Uwchmynydd and Bardsey from Rhiw

corrugated building on the right, there is a parking place on the right in front of the next chapel by the phone box.

A few yards west of the phone box take the cul-de-sac lane on the right, ignoring the signed footpath that shortly goes up to the right keep straight ahead through a farm gate into an open field. Follow the farm lane round past the farmhouse and rounding a bend the lane divides, one branch turning back on itself to the farm, the other bearing right to two more farms, but we take the waymarked grass track in front through a gate down a very short grass lane into a field. Following round the left-hand side of the field making for a gap into the next field with another white cottage across the valley in front. Heading

The first lane which you take from the car park

towards this we come to a stile in the far left corner with a bracken covered path down to a stream and up to the garden gate of the cottage named Pennant. A Celtic cross marker (marking the pilgrims' route) points right and we follow the fence along until progress is barred by a fence after 250 yards. There seems to be a stile missing but it is fairly easy to negotiate the fence on the left and keeping the fence on the left another in the top left corner out onto the open ground beyond. In the absence of a specific path follow the line of the fence on the left steeply uphill. Where the fence veers off left do likewise but keep climbing to a rocky knoll and rounding the shoulder of the main hill drop down to a green wall in the depression. Follow this for a few paces and where it goes off left keep straight ahead up the hill to emerge suddenly onto a narrow concrete road. This takes us up to the now abandoned coastguard lookout on top of Mynydd Mawr.

Descend from the summit by a concrete footpath and steps and follow the grass path to the left which takes us round the hillside where we can see down in front the outline of a former building. We cross this field to a gully leading down to the sea at the bottom of which is Ffynnon Fair (*St Mary's Well*). It is covered at high water but the fresh water bubbles through – it is not easy to find. Returning now up the gully there are, on the right, two small fenced enclosures where the National Trust are carrying out plant research, but just before the second we take the track that leads up the next hill, Mynydd Gwyddel. Following one of the many sheep tracks either round the shoulder or over the top we make, in a south-easterly direction for a stile in the corner down below at the head of the narrow inlet Porth Felen. Keeping to the seaward side of this field another stile takes us out onto the open headlands.

Here keep to the top side of the open ground where just before the fence in front there are two gates on the left, the one on the right leads onto a green lane. Follow this up, past two cottages on the left where it becomes tarmac. Continue straight ahead and in 500 yards take the first road on the left (not the rough lane before the farm.) ¾ mile down this road turn right at the T-junction and the car should be in front.

Originally in: *Llŷn Peninsula Coastal Walks*, Richard A. R. Quine

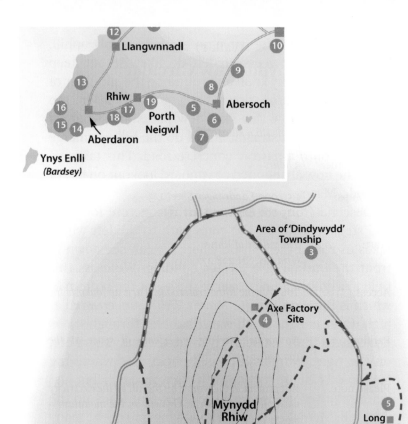

Walk 17
Mynydd Rhiw Circular

Walk details
Approx distance: *4 miles/6.4 kilometres*

Approx time: *3 hours*

O.S. Maps: 1:50 000 *Landranger Sheet 123*
                  1:25 000 *Explorer Sheet 253*

Start: *The village of Rhiw*
                  Grid Ref. SH 228 277

Access: *Towards the Rhiw crossroads. Turn up towards the*
                  Village Hall.

Parking: *No formal parking but plenty of space at the*
                  roadside.

Please note: *Wet ground in the winter on the hill by the electricity*
                  mast on Mynydd Rhiw. Growth on the mountain –
                  mostly gorse and bracken.

Going: *Quiet lanes.*

This walk is quite a mixture, with pleasant country
lanes and old houses, pretty scenery and mountain
strolls. Quite a tiring walk but worth the effort.

Walk directions
Take the road towards Rhiw crossroads and at these
turn right (left if coming from Aberdaron) heading
through the village and past the village hall on the left.
   Carry on, following the road to the left.

The chapel at Rhiw

In about 200 metres there is a road to your right and on the other side of the road, a stone stile, cross this and follow the footpath leading around the hillside.

This path carries on for about ½ a mile and passes through areas of old mine workings from the manganese mines (1).

At the end of this section make towards the corner of the field and over the stone step stile in the drystone wall. Turn right here onto a green lane (2).

Leave the green lane on the left after about 50 metres through a field gate and keeping to the wall on your left, head along this path until it approaches the road at a bend. As a marker you will be about 90 degrees to the radio mast on Mynydd Rhiw. Also on the opposite side of the road is a house called 'Glwyd'.

Turn right onto the road and proceed along this for a fair distance, until the first right turn which will take you steadily uphill past a cluster of houses with fine views to your left (3).

Continue on up the hill, nearing the highest point on the road at the sign for the 'National Trust', opposite a large outcrop of rock, at this point if you would like a detour to the Neolithic axe factory on the eastern flanks of Mynydd Rhiw take the path up the hillside on your right, and along the flank of the mountain can be seen some areas of loose stone, there are the remains of the axe factory (4).

Retrace your steps to the road heading roughly in the direction of Rhiw with the large crescent of Porth Neigwl (Hell's Mouth Bay) sweeping into the distance.

After a short descent passing a cottage on the right called Heather, look for a lane leading off to the left with several names and post boxes including Bryn-y-Ffynnon. After turning into this lane make your way downhill until the lane passes some open ground on the left and on the right is an old farm. Just after the cottage is a well, it is not named but is fairly large, about 3 metres square; continue along the path to the next cottage called Tan-y-Muriau. Just before you reach this cottage you will see on your right a long cairn or burial mound. (5).

Below the muriau is a sunken path, now overgrown, but you can walk beside it to the track, turn right and follow this path through a couple of gates until you emerge onto the road, turn right here and continue uphill passing on the way a house called Tyn-y-Graig (6).

On reaching the T-junction with the Rhiw – Sarn road at the church, turn left and follow this road back in to Rhiw. As you walk uphill look into the fields on your left just in front of a large white house where you

The village and Mynydd Rhiw beyond

will see the remains of another cromlech, similar, though not as large as the one just visited (7).

At T-junction turn left towards the car.

Detour

As you reach the cottage Pen-y-Groes where you have parked your car and provided that you have a bit more energy left, carry on down the main road past the cottage on your left called Tan-y-Bwlch and turn left into a track next to a large white house called Llwynfor and beside the drive into the house is another lower one that leads into a field where just across the stream there is another long cairn or muriau, described later.

Retrace your steps to your car remembering to shut all gates.

History notes

1. The manganese mines visible here were worked at

the same time in conjunction with those at Nant-y-Gadwen (nr. Rhiw). There is a homestead settlement, the remains of which are visible with a little imagination, just the other side of the field wall at the end of the mine workings. There are field terracings which are associated with this hut group but they are virtually ploughed out. There are further terracings on the hillside, where there is also another hut circle, but thick gorse and heather now conceal them from view. The settlements here probably date from the Dark Age up to medieval times.

2. On the rising spur of land to the left at this point is a concentric banked enclosure, the two banks form circles of 95 metres and 70 metres, they are only visible on the ground as slight swellings about 33 cms high and 3 metres wide. Locals recall removal of stones from these walls in recent years. A central feature is reputedly visible from air photographs and is probably the site of a dwelling. A writer in 1696 records a stone circle in this area and it is possible that this central feature represents the last trace of this. There is nothing else in the neighbourhood to which this description could apply. This double ring-work construction probably dates from the pre-Roman Iron Age c.100 BC, it is likely to be contemporary with other similar constructions on Llŷn e.g. Castell Caeron, Conion, and Pen-y-Gaer near Abersoch.

3. This section of closely-associated smallholdings is a fine example of the continuation of use into modern times of an area designated as a township possibly as early as the 12th century. The township was called 'Dindywydd'. The sites of the existing cottages are

likely to be on the same sites as the original medieval dwellings. Two cottages remain with names harking back to this period, Brondywydd and Penydref (head of the township). There was a local tradition extant earlier in the present century that a disaster took place here. It seems that a love-lorn poet wandering in the area came to the township and asked for alms, he was refused and sent packing, he strongly resented this rebuttal and as he left he uttered a curse on the place which shortly after was destroyed by fire. Dindywydd was a 'bond vill' paying its dues and tributes to the 'maerdref' or 'Llys' of Neigwl (a maerdref or Llys is the dwelling place of the 'overlord' of the area). Just over the hill behind the house called 'Pen-y-Castell' is another concentric ring-work fort of Celtic date although virtually nothing now remains visible.

4. The first farming communities reached Britain around 3500 BC in the Neolithic Age. Some of these people arrived by way of the Irish sea route and settled on the shores of Wales and Ireland. it is possible that the Neolithic period is as old on the Welsh coast as anywhere else in Britain. Very little remains as evidence of these early people in Llŷn except a few burial sites, some of which are quite impressive. There is however one other important site dating from the Neolithic – the stone-axe factory on the north-east slope of Mynydd Rhiw. This site was first recognised as an axe factory in 1956 when it was revealed by extensive gorse-burning. The site consists of five roughly circular hollows in a line about 90 metres long and bearing 40 degrees these hollows are the remains of an open cast mining system following a vein of suitable rock, the largest hollow at the north east end

Rhiw church

is about 16 metres across, the others vary between 4.5 metres and 7.5 metres across. The banks surrounding the hollows are composed of the waste product of flaking. It seems likely that the quarrying only took place in the summer months, during the winter the people would have lived lower down the mountain side in a permanent community although nothing has been found to indicate where this may have been. It is possible that the factory workers may have lived on the site during the summer months as one of the hollows, on excavation showed evidence of two hearths. The date of these original workings may be as early as 3000 BC. Two further hearths were discovered within the same hollow as the two previous but on a much higher level above the much silted-over earlier hearths, a tentative date in the 12th century BC, has been assigned to the later hearths. This clearly shows that the factory was in use for many centuries and spanned the period of the Neolithic and early Bronze Ages. It is interesting that the later quarrying work seems to have been undertaken with less skill and attention to use of rock-type than the earlier.

Axe factories such as this (there are several around Britain), provide good evidence of an extensive and widespread trading system in this remote period, as tools produced at the various sites which are petrologically identifiable show up in widely dispersed regions. Tools from Mynydd Rhiw have been found all over Wales and the Marches, while those from another axe factory at Craig Lwyd, also in Caernarfonshire, near Llanfairfechan, have been found in southern England and even on the Continent. This distribution implies a fairly advanced trading infrastructure. In the case of Mynydd Rhiw it appears that a range of tool-types were produced, including small delicate knives, scrapers, hand axes of various sizes, adzes and large tree-felling axes. Although trade has been established involving these products it may be that most of them were reserved for local use.

5. This cromlech or 'long cairn' as it is more usually described, is, like the axe factory described above, of Neolithic date, indeed it is highly likely that it is the work of the same culture involved with the quarrying. The cromlech consists of a mound of loose stone about 27 metres long and 6 metres wide with a small ruined chamber at the north west end, and a larger chamber standing apart further to the north east. It is possible that the larger chamber was included in the mound of stones but that they have been removed to construct the field boundary. The structure can be visualised as consisting of two (or three) chambers containing burials with the whole covered by a mound of stone, there may have been a passage giving access to the interior of the mound on the south west side. This monument falls into the general class of 'chambered tombs', they are present, often with characteristic regional differences throughout the whole of Britain. They demonstrate the almost universally similar burial customs of the peoples inhabiting Britain in the Neolithic period. Although these structures are generally considered to be funerary monuments it is quite likely that they had a wider role in the community. In fact it may be helpful to consider them as having a similar function to a church. The church, for us, as well as being a place of burial, is also a place of worship, it is often a communal centre and focus, a source of communal pride, a place of security and sanctuary, the sacred ground of the community. The Neolithic cromlechs and passage graves were undoubtedly the most permanent and impressive buildings, with by far the most effort and man-hours invested in them – they are still with us 5000 years after their construction. It would seem then that these

monuments had a deep awe-inspiring religious significance, and a little imagination at this site can conjure up a scene with the silent members of the community witnessing the ritual internment of a beloved chief, a moving ceremony performed by the tribal shaman who would wait, maybe with a few of the chief's close relatives, for the time of sunset, and when it dips close to the horizon, and the hillside is bathed in ruddy gold, the spirit of the dead chief rises and leaves its earthly tomb through the open south-west passage to greet his ancestors once again and walk in splendour behind the setting sun.

6. Tyn-y-Graig – this cottage, built in 1762 (there is an inscription cut into the face of the east wall: WWI/1762, probably for William Williams, the owner and his wife who in 1776, lived at Plas yn Rhiw). There is reason to believe that, in spite of the date inscription that the house is earlier, say early 18th century, this evidence come from the plan and the nature and quality of construction of the woodwork inside. The house today retains almost all of its character, it is nice to see an old Welsh cottage neither derelict nor 'modernised' out of all recognition.

7. In the sloping field to the left of the road at this point is another complex system of old huts and fields. Surrounding these features are numerous remains of contemporary field boundaries. These long huts may be of a later date than the round huts. If, for sake of argument, the round hut systems are dated to the late-Roman period and early Dark Ages c.400-700 AD, it may be that the long huts represent the period of the later Dark Ages c.700-1100 AD. It cannot be

emphasised too often that it is impossible to be accurate with dates for huts in general and these dates are only intended to be a guide.

Selection of original walk, originally published in:
Walks in the Llŷn Peninsula
Part 1: South and West

by N. Burras and J. Stiff

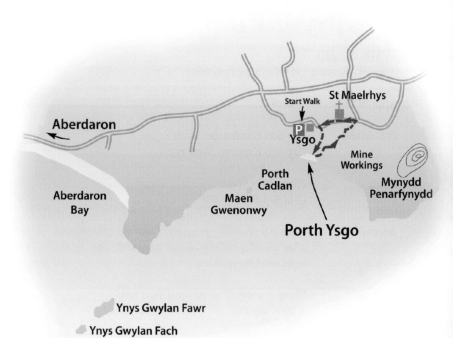

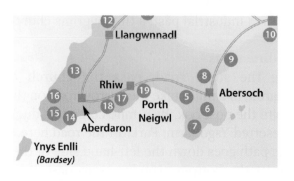

Walk 18
Porth Ysgo

Walk details
Approx distance: 1½ *miles/2.4 kilometres*

Approx time: *¾ hour*

O.S. Maps: *1:50 000 Landranger Sheet 123*
                  1:25 000 Explorer Sheet 253

Start: *Fferm Ysgo*
                  Grid Ref. SH 207 268

Access: *From Aberdaron – go up road past the church, and after about 2 miles look out for Porth Ysgo to the right near the post box.*

Parking: *There is a small car park on Ysgo farm. A fee is payable.*

Please note: *Very steep steps down to Porth Ysgo beach.*

Going: *Path and country lane.*

Short but worthwhile walk to a lovely cove; reminders of the area industrial past; a tiny pilgrims church.

Walk directions
Taking the steep road, pass the church out of Aberdaron, in 2 miles take the narrow road on the right opposite the post box. In ½ mile come to a duck pond and deserted Ysgo farm. Park off the road here.

The path goes down the left-hand side of the valley where, at the bottom, wooden steps descend to this

Porth Ysgo

St Maelrhys, Porth Ysgo

small sandy bay. Returning to the path we carry on round the hillside into the next valley Nant y Gadwen.

Ahead will be seen the spoil heaps of the manganese mines which operated in this area from the mid-19th century until 1946. The path carries on up the valley through a kissing gate. The main mine shaft is up on the right just before the path crosses a stone footbridge, but take care, it is unfenced. The path shortly comes out on a lane. Turn left to return to the car on the way passing the tiny church of St Maelrhys.

Originally published in:
Llŷn Peninsula Coastal Walks

by Richard A. R. Quine

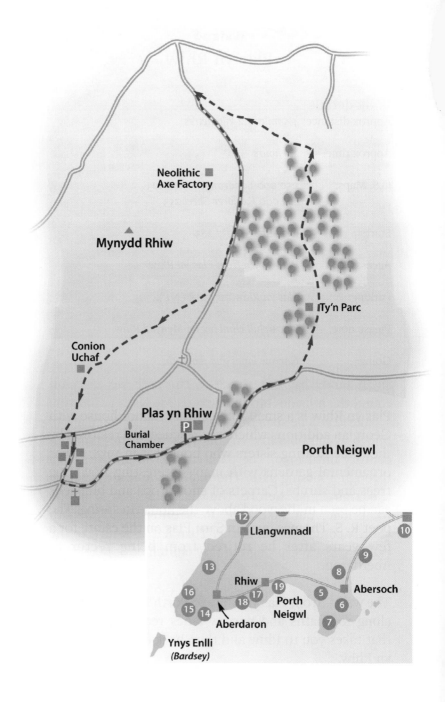

Walk 19
Plas yn Rhiw

Walk details

Approx distance: *4½ miles/7.2 kilometres*

Approx time: *2½ hours*

O.S. Maps: *1:50 000 Landranger Sheet 123*
                1:25 000 Explorer Sheet 253

Start: *Grid Ref. SH 237 283*

Access: *Walk down from Plas yn Rhiw.*

Parking: *Plas yn Rhiw car park (NT).*

Please note: *Sme uphill climbing on Mynydd Rhiw.*

Going: *Narrow lanes and footpaths.*

Plas yn Rhiw is a small 16th century manor house with Georgian additions which was rescued and restored by the three Keating sisters who bought it in 1938. It has ornamental gardens with many interesting flowering trees and shrubs. Carpets of snowdrops and bluebells can be seen in the wood above the house in spring. The poet R. S. Thomas lived in Sarn Plas on the estate for a few years after he retired from being rector of Aberdaron.

The walk – from Plas yn Rhiw to Porth Neigwl and then along footpaths and narrow lanes reaching the road that takes you to Rhiw and then back downhill to Plas yn Rhiw.

The summer garden at Plas yn Rhiw

Park your car in Plas yn Rhiw. (There is a bus service to Rhiw, and you can start the walk from there.) After visiting the house, walk out of the grounds and go down the hill until you reach the bottom with a caravan park on your right and a farm on your left.

You will then come to a Public Footpath sign on your right which leads you over a stile to Porth Neigwl. It will take you about ten minutes to go to the beach from here – well worth a visit.

Otherwise, carry on along the road until you come to another Public Footpath sign and the sign to Ty'n Parc. Follow this path or track to the left, past Ty'n Parc and into a pine forest. Carry on past some sheds on your right until you come to a clear patch in the forest and a track running into it from the left. Go straight ahead along a narrow path towards a white house until you come to a gate.

Go through the gate and up the path through the brambles behind a house called Tyddyn Corn until you come to another gate. Go through it and up the track, then left through the trees. Go out of the trees and near a gate take the track to its left (i.e. the one in the middle). Pass the white house on the left and go up the path to the right to a gate and a broken stile. Go through the gate and walk alongside the wall until you come to two houses on your left.

Turn left past the nearest house until you come to a

track and follow it to the right until you come to a cattle grid and a tarmaced road. Go past two houses on your left until you come to a junction and a telephone kiosk. Turn left and up the hill past a stile on your left to the top of the hill where there is a magnificent view to your left of Porth Neigwl and the southern Llŷn coast. To your right is Mynydd Rhiw.

Carry on until you come to, on your right, a gate, a corrugated iron shed and a stone stile. Go over the stile and follow the track to the left until you come to two gates and a stile to their right. Go over the stile and follow the path that eventually turns into a track and then joins another track and forward towards some houses. Walk towards the gate, go through it and near a house called Hirael you will reach a crossroads. Turn left and then right at the next crossroads and into Rhiw.

Walk past the village hall on your right and to the crossroads. Turn left and go down the hill towards Porth Neigwl. After walking a few minutes you will see Bwlch cottage on your left. Carry on down the hill and near the bottom, on your left, you will see the sign to Plas yn Rhiw and return to your car.

Other Points of Interest
Bwlch, formerly known as Bwlch y Rhiw – was the home of Morgan Griffith or Morgan y Gogrwr (the sieve maker) who was an 18th century nonconformist preacher. At that time every preacher had to be licensed by the church –

Porth Neigwl from Plas yn Rhiw

February snowdrops at Plas yn Rhiw

and Griffith was not. He was twice caught preaching in the fields and the second time was taken to court in Pwllheli. To try and get him a lighter sentence, his brother-in-law brought his two children – in baskets on a mule – to the courthouse but to no avail. Because his children could read, it was assumed that he was teaching them 'bad things'. Griffith was found guilty and sent to the navy. Sometime in the early 1740s he was put on the Colchester which was anchored in the Thames. Britain was at war with France at the time and the Colchester went up to Scotland to patrol the waters there. Conditions were very bad on the ship and eventually Griffith, like many others, died and was buried at sea.

Mynydd Rhiw There are the remains of a Neolithic stone axe factory on its northern slope, a burial chamber on its eastern side and the remains of an old homestead on the southern side. There are old manganese mines at the foot of the mountain, where over 60,000 tons of ore were mined during the Second World War. It was taken by an aerial ropeway to a pier on the shore. During the beginning of the 20th century (especially in 1912, during the Russian/Japanese War), this area produced 90% of Britain's manganese, employing 200 men. It was used to harden steel in Brymbo, in north-eastern Wales, and was used in the production of armaments. At the end if the 19th century, the ore would be carried in small trucks to a stream where it would be washed by women and then transported on sledges to Porth Neigwl to be loaded onto ships. On the top of the hill is a radio station tracking missiles which are fired from Aberporth on the Ceredigion coast.

Porth Neigwl (or Hell's Mouth) – has seen numerous shipwrecks over the centuries. In 1629 a French ship carrying members of the aristocracy, lured by lights carried by wreckers on the shore, hit the rocks. It is said that the locals attacked the survivors, killing them and cutting their fingers and ears off to get at the jewellery. Two local men were hanged for this foul deed. In 1865, an Austrian ship carrying corn went on the rocks and its cargo was spread over the area. It is said that local farms gathered it all up and fed it to their pigs. In 1898, a ship called *The Twelve Apostles*, which had been built at Pwllheli in 1858, was blown ashore and the captain's message to Lloyds of London read '*Twelve Apostles* taking water in Hell's Mouth'. The crew managed to get into a small boat but got into difficulties. The maid of nearby Trefollwyn saw them and waded into the stormy water to help bring the boat ashore. Such is the ferocity of the weather at Porth Neigwl that during the last century a paint manufacturer put up painted frames on the eastern end of the bay to test the durability of the paint. These frames have now either corroded or fallen into the sea.

Originally published in:
National Trust Walks 1. Northern Wales

by Dafydd Meirion

First published in 2012

© original authors/Llygad Gwalch

© Carreg Gwalch 2012

ISBN: 978-1-84524-194-0

Cover design: Carreg Gwalch
Cover image: Traeth Penllech

Gwasg Carreg Gwalch,
12 Iard yr Orsaf, Llanrwst, Wales LL26 0EH
tel: 01492 642031
fax: 01492 641502
email: books@carreg-gwalch.com
website: www.carreg-gwalch.com

Also in
the
series: